1. John Slidell

2. Nicholas Trist

3. John C. Fremont

4. David Stockton

5. Stephen Kreaney

Gadsden purchase

1. Bought from Santa Anna
2. Now New Mexico / Arizona
3. Paid 10$ million

Bennett's Angel

Other books by Barton A. Midwood

Bodkin
Phantoms
The Nativity

BENNETT'S ANGEL

a novel

Barton A. Midwood

Paris Review Editions

Copyright 1989 by Barton A. Midwood
All rights reserved
including the right of reproduction
in whole or in part in any form
Published by Paris Review Editions
British American Publishing
3 Cornell Road
Latham, NY 12110
Manufactured in the United States of America

94 93 92 91 90 5 4 3 2 1

Library of Congress Cataloging in Publication Data

Midwood, Barton A., 1938–
    Bennett's angel / Barton A. Midwood.
    p.   cm.
    ISBN 0-945167-15-6 : $17.95
    I. Title.
PS3563.I37B46   1989
813'.54—dc19   88-38758
                                                   CIP

for Laura Melim-Midwood

Socrates: Then it is a fact, Simmias, that true philosophers make dying their profession, and that to them of all men death is least alarming.

PHAEDO, Plato

Chapters

1. Map
2. A City, a Man
3. Fisher and Bennett in the Plymouth
4. True Professions

Contents

MAP

It was not 1959. It was not a cold November. It was not a small college town in New York, and he was not twenty-one. In fact, he was not even David Bennett. He was someone else altogether, someone in another time and another place, though who and when and where escape him as soon as he wakes up, for the instant he opens his eyes, he sees bad weather in the room. He sees two lampshades rocking and the curtains bellied like sails, he sees rain on the rug and lightning on the wall, and he is compelled to get out of bed at once and hurry across the room to shut the window.

This done, he wipes the rain from his face with his sleeve and concludes that, no matter what may have been the case in his dream, his runaway dream now receding into an impenetrable mire, at the moment it is 1959, that it is a cold November, that it is a small college town in New York, and that he is absolutely David Bennett and no other.

But still he is troubled by a vague sense that the morning is not what it ought to be, so he turns his back on the closed window and, lowering his eyes, conjures up a map, a deep and colorful map of the previous day; and therein he discovers the cause of his difficulty; namely, that at the top, in the corner, where the night lies pictured like an arctic sea, a piece is missing.

This can't be, he thinks, for his memory has never before let him down as badly as this, and at the same time he scans the map, supposing that if only he strikes an attitude of right concentration, the piece that is missing is bound to proceed, in short order, out of the piece that is there.

In response the map shimmers and animates, and he sees himself at the edge of the night.

He sees himself as an actor on a stage, playing the part of a hero who came to a bad end. He was wearing a false beard, brown and close-cropped. His voice was caustic and fierce. He stood before a gallows, among ten other actors. One corner of the dark backdrop glowed with a faint red light to suggest a distant fire. Words were exchanged, lyric and high toned. He stepped up on the gallows, and a rope was put around his neck. The lights went down. He hurried into the wings and watched in silence, as the lights came up

2

again, and the final scene was played without him, a brief, dispassionate scene, after which the curtain closed, then opened again at once.

One person in the audience applauded. He applauded enthusiastically, standing up in the center aisle at the rear, and shouted, "Bravo," and other things as well. This was the director, Anthony Dicataldo. Dicataldo had hollow cheeks and eyesockets, and his hair was black. Nearby sat the assistant director with a script in his hand, smiling. The assistant had a fat face and wore eyeglasses and a hearing aid. The rest of the seats, about five hundred, were empty. The whole cast and crew assembled on the stage. Dicataldo announced that he had a few comments, but that he would make them tomorrow night before the performance. Meanwhile, he said, they should all go home and get a good night's rest. Then, on a note of praise, he dismissed the company with a wave of the hand, adding that he would like a few words with Bennett before he left the theater.

Bennett retreated backstage to the dressing room and tore off the beard. He removed the glue from his face with a sharp solvent and washed the powder off with soap and water. He got out of his costume and into his ordinary clothes. The costume, which was drenched in sweat, he stuffed into a canvas airline bag; then he hurried out front and up the aisle to Dicataldo. The cast and crew were still onstage, milling about, cheerful and spirited.

Dicataldo, rising from his seat, commended Bennett on a good performance, then offered one suggestion: that Bennett slow his pace in the love scene in the

3

middle of the second act, particularly his delivery of a long speech they had come to call "the raindrop speech," in which the main idea was that every raindrop is an analogue of the world. Dicataldo was partial to the raindrop speech, he said, and he wanted the audience to have time to take it in. As Bennett was the author of the play and likewise partial to the raindrop speech, he took the suggestion in good part and responded with a silent nod. After a pause, Dicataldo proposed that the two of them go somewhere and have a beer, but Bennett hesitated, then declined, and immediately a shadow of resentment fell across Dicataldo's face. In an attempt to ease the mood, Bennett explained that he was tired and worked up and needed to be alone, but Dicataldo turned away, aloof and morose, and, sitting down, began to devote exclusive attention to the assistant, talking in a confidential undertone and pointing at a list of comments in blue ink clipped to the script in the assistant's lap.

With a shrug of the shoulders, Bennett walked off and went out to the lobby. He paused at the front door and held his breath for a moment. He had his airline bag in his hand. He stepped outside. It was early evening. In front of the theater were four shallow steps, a broad expanse of concrete, and then a black tarmac road. Parked at the curb was a 1955 white Buick convertible with the top up. The top was dark green canvas and faded. As he walked down the steps, the door on the passenger side was pushed open from within. Bennett went over and put both hands on the canvas top and ducked his head to look at the driver.

The driver was alone in the car. With a weary smile, he told Bennett to get in, and Bennett did so without

4

hesitation, sitting in the passenger seat with his left foot in the car and his right foot on the curb.

"Shut the door," said the driver. "I'm freezing to death."

Bennett swung his right foot from the curb into the car and shut the door. Through the window he saw Dicataldo, who had come out of the theater and was standing at the head of the four shallow steps in a long black coat, both hands in his pockets, a script tucked under one arm. His eyes, furious and intense, met Bennett's.

The driver turned the ignition key and started the engine, which roared like an outboard motor on a boat, then diminished to a soft hum.

As the car pulled slowly away from the curb, Bennett glanced back through the rear window at his bicycle, a three-speed English racer with a burnished gold frame, chained to a rack. In the rack were three other bicycles as well.

"You're going to have to drive me back here to pick up my bike when we're done," he said. "I need it first thing in the morning to go to the laundromat and wash my costume."

In the next few hours Bennett and the driver of the Buick went to three bars. The first bar was local; the other two were in a small town about six miles down the highway. In each of the three bars Bennett had one beer, and in the third bar he also had half a glass of brandy. The driver of the Buick had only brandy, six glasses in all, but they appeared to have little effect.

Bennett and the driver of the Buick were fellowship students in a special graduate program in the humanities which was designed to bypass the master's degree and lead directly to a doctorate. They were both now in their second year. The driver of the Buick was the oldest in the program, and Bennett was the youngest.

As an undergraduate, Bennett had completed a four-year bachelor of arts program in three years, by attending summer sessions and carrying a heavy course load. With a major in comparative literature and minors in German and Latin, he graduated with honors at the age of twenty, winning a federal grant that covered tuition for graduate school as well as living expenses. This grant he experienced as luxury and liberation. In his undergraduate years he had attended a college near the home of his parents, and he lived with them. Though the parents were good to him, he was an only child, and as soon as he entered his freshman year, he began to experience a terrible intensification of his long-standing wish for brothers and sisters, with whom he might share some of the parental good, because this good, while not bad, had gotten to be far more than he knew what to do with. Also, in those days, though he was on scholarship, the scholarship covered only tuition, and he had been obliged to work on weekends in the stockroom of a local supermarket to earn money for other expenses. In graduate school the situation was different. Now he attended a college several hundred miles from the home of his parents, and as the fellowship grant provided funds well beyond the cost of tuition, he was able to afford an apartment of his own, and he had his weekends free, free mainly to read novels, dark European novels, from dawn to midnight. He even managed to put aside a few hundred dollars of the grant money in a savings account.

As for the driver of the Buick, he was married and had a little daughter and a taste for certain expensive things, and for him the grant was not enough. To earn extra money he taught one section of freshman logic, three hours a week. Also, as he was a veteran of the Korean War, in which he had served as an ordinary foot soldier in the infantry, he received some financial help by way of the GI Bill. All in all, between the grant, the logic, and the GI Bill, he managed to get by. On weekends, which he too, like Bennett, had free, usually he shut himself up in a carrel in the library ten or twelve hours a day to work on a doctoral thesis, and by now he had finished all but the last chapter. Among the eighteen other students in the program, by contrast, none had yet begun their theses, and most had not even picked a topic. The rate at which he had produced the work, in fact, was both suspect and unprecedented in the department. Though his special interests included both mathematics and philosophy, he had made no attempt to wed them in the thesis. According to the few students who had seen bits of it, the thesis, titled *Murder as a Reasonable Imperative,* was purely philosophic, was located in the field of ethics, and, being devoid of number, owed to mathematics only a certain sense of cunning and surprise.

In Bennett's perception the driver of the Buick, though just twenty-seven, had the aspect of an old man, in virtue obviously not of his years, but of some essential quality, which the fact of his youth only brought into sharper relief. He was just under medium height. Though somewhat bent in the spine, he carried himself tilted back from the waist and with his chin up. His shoulders were broad, his waist narrow, his legs short. His hands were large and powerful, the fingers knotted at the joints, the nails nicely manicured. His hair was light brown with gold highlights, receding at the temples and thin on top and combed into a widow's peak. His cheekbones were high and prominent, his eyes grayish green and potent and slanted, his teeth perfect and false. His ears had long pendulous lobes and were pointed at the top. His skin was deep olive and sleek and usually had the spicy scent of an aftershave lotion; but even without the lotion, he radiated an air of aristocratic cleanliness, and all his movements were slow and studied, as if executed in a medium thicker than air.

Last night, as on all public occasions, the cut and condition of his clothes were immaculate. He had been dressed in a tweed jacket, a light blue shirt with a starched collar open at the throat, brown woolen trousers, and brown loafers with pointed toes.

His name was Dimitri Leskov. The story of this name was the very last thing Bennett remembered of the night. Leskov had told it out of the blue. As far as Bennett could see, nothing in the previous conversation, or in the situation around them in the bar, had suggested such a story. This trick was typical of Leskov, and in fact, on this particular occasion, the trick was done in a manner less alarming than usual.

Usually he launched into a new topic right in the middle of a sentence, or with a startling question, as if he were merely continuing aloud some spectral conversation that had been going on all along in the air around him independently of the spoken conversation actually in progress. This time, however, he did not begin in the middle of a sentence, or with a startling question. In fact, though his tone was comic and bleak and somewhat poisonous, he began almost modestly with a simple declaration.

Dimitri Leskov was a name that signified something he was not, he said.

And this, he added perversely, was significant.

And then, after a pause, he told the story, a story about his name, and about his father.

His father's first name, he said, was Ivan. But before his father was Ivan, he was Yitzak. When he was Yitzak, he lived in Russia, in a small Jewish village, near Odessa. And if life were not a fairy tale, and if six giants had not walked into his house on the crisp Easter Sunday morning of 1913, and slaughtered his parents and sister, he would have been Yitzak to this day. His sister Rivka they strangled with a shoelace and cooked like a goose in the oven. The mother too they strangled, but they did not cook her, because the oven was full. The father they did not kill. They just broke his legs and hands with a hammer and cut his tongue out and tossed him out the window; but after they left, he crawled on his elbows and knees across the yard to the well and drowned himself.

On this day Yitzak had been away in Odessa, where he had gone to buy a new coat for his sister, and to sell some onions and eggs and two geese, and also to deliver six pairs of boots that his father had made to order for some officials in the civil service. When he returned home a week later, he got the story from the neighbors, who got it from two stupid cheder boys, who had hidden in back of the house and watched the massacre through a crack in the wall. Five neighbors and also the rabbi went with Yitzak to the graves to say the prayer for the dead. The family was already buried, and the funeral had been made. The graves were marked with sticks of pine, which bore the names inscribed on little plates of brass. On the grave of his sister, Yitzak laid the new coat and poured oil on it and burned it. Then he went to his house and shaved his beard and cut his earlocks and left the village. He was at this time twenty years old. He set off on foot, back to Odessa, to find passage to America. On the road he stopped to eat at a tavern, where a group of soldiers regarded him suspiciously and asked his name. On the spur of the moment Yitzak invented the name Ivan Leskov. Where he got this name he had no idea. In all his life he never knew a Leskov. No doubt he had heard it at some time, but he could not remember when, nor could he reason out why this particular name, rather than any other, should be the first to spring to his mind. To him it seemed that he had gotten it out of thin air, and as the suspicion vanished from the eyes of the soldiers as soon as the name was uttered, it straightway had for him the quality of magic.

Later, when he was in the filthy crowded steerage section of a steamship bound for America with a few hundred other refugees, he got some new ideas about the name from a fellow passenger by the name of Yussel. Whenever Dimitri Leskov's father told the story of the name, he identified this Yussel always with the same epithet: "a crazy pockmarked anarchist, all skin and bones, who dragged with him everywhere a potato sack full of books, as if it were his own mother."

"If a Jew wants a name that is not the name of a Jew," said Yussel, "Leskov is not bad. This is because of Nikolai Leskov."

"Who is this Nikolai Leskov?" said Yitzak.

"He was a writer who understood The Jewish Question. He even wrote a story about it. Actually the story is about a Russian, who hates Rumanians; but if you read between the lines, you can see it is about The Jewish Question."

"If this Nikolai Leskov understood The Jewish Question," said Yitzak, "he should have written about Jews, not Rumanians."

"You have a point," said Yussel, "but all the same, you are a stupid man," and he took up his sack of books and went to the other side of the ship and refused to speak to Yitzak again for the rest of the voyage.

The brief conversation had an effect, however, and when Yitzak arrived in America and settled in a noisy Jewish ghetto near the Boston shipyards, though his Hebrew name was no longer a danger to his life, he became Ivan Leskov once and for all, a name that now had for him not only magic, but also, thanks to Yussel, the scent of good will and protection. Ironically, by the Irish community in Boston, the name

11

Leskov, like all Russian and Polish names, was often mistaken for Jewish anyway, and this allowed him to live with the name in good conscience. After all, he did not wish to escape the liability of a Jewish name altogether, as had some of his fellow immigrants, who had taken up names like Brown and Smith and Miller.

"Some even took up names like Bennett," added Leskov, with a grin.

Beyond this satiric remark, which concluded the story of Ivan Leskov and his name, the next morning Bennett could remember very little. He could remember picking up his glass of brandy and gazing at it, he could remember a burst of coarse laughter suddenly issuing from a few patrons in a far corner of the room, and, more significantly, he could remember a fleeting thought about his own father, who, like Ivan Leskov, also had two names, his present name and a common Hebrew name he had been born with. Since Bennett had never had occasion to tell anyone at the college the story of his father and the two names, however, Leskov's remark had the invasive quality of a mystical insight, and Bennett was offended.

He was offended, first, because the remark was a direct insult to his own father, and, second, because the remark appeared to suggest that Bennett himself had something to hide, and that Leskov had seen it. But, as Bennett felt he had nothing to hide, he felt as well that there was nothing to see; and therefore, he experienced the suggestion as unjust.

The remark appeared also to suggest that, in the case of his own father, the escape from one name to another had been impelled, not by unequivocal danger, as had been the case with Leskov's father, but by shame, and that the escape had itself been a shameful act, and that Bennett did not know this. But he did know. Didn't he know? Of course! He knew it as well as anyone! Nevertheless, since he was not the one who had initiated the escape, in his opinion he himself had nothing whatever to be ashamed of!

On a more difficult level, Leskov's remark, coming as it did at the end of a tale of hatred and horror, insinuated in Bennett's mind the idea that his identity as a Jew was a thing which he might, after all, and with reason, want to hide. And since this idea was one he had not previously considered with much attention, its sudden emergence out of an offense to his dignity confused and overwhelmed him. In an attempt to get his bearings, he picked up the glass of brandy and gazed at it, as the blood burned in his cheeks, and a host of unfamiliar passions of some force took him by the throat.

Whether he spoke out or kept silent, however, the next morning he could not remember. He could not even remember whether or not he drank the brandy. Beyond the moment of offense, the passions at his throat, and the large delicate glass in his hand, he could remember nothing, nothing whatever.

All the same, he tried. He tried as hard as he could. Standing in his bedroom, he fixed his eyes on the carpet and searched his imaginary map of yesterday, looking here, and looking there, but in all the minutes and latitudes of the day and the night, he could find no clue to the nature or whereabouts of the forgotten episode, which had escaped him, apparently, in much the same way as had the dream out of which he just woke.

On several occasions in the past, a dream forgotten in the morning had come back to him in the afternoon, invariably as a graceful surprise, lighting up spontaneously, sparked by some otherwise insignificant commonplace—a phrase in a conversation, a gesture, an ordinary object—and he now wished that something similar might occur with the forgotten episode of the previous night, in exchange for which he was ready to give the memory of a thousand dreams, of all the dreams he ever dreamed.

So many dreams, though, may be too many to give, he thought, and his readiness to give them might itself be an obstacle to getting the thing he wanted in return; so it might be wise to put his readiness aside, or, in a more devious vein, to disguise his readiness, perhaps as apathy, pretending to forget that he had forgotten, and in this way seduce the fugitive memory into coming back of its own accord. Still, a seduction like this could be abysmal, and suddenly he feared, on second thought, that he might go too far, pretend with too much zeal, get absolutely taken in by his own pretense, and then, in the end, after failing altogether to seduce the fugitive memory into coming back, find himself in a condition of blithe serenity, going about his business with a tidy smile and an eye to the future, completely unaware that any memory of the least importance had escaped in the first place!—which prospect struck him as catastrophic, a state of affairs that would reduce him to a kind of idiot.

14

In the face of this alarming prospect of idiocy, he renewed his effort to remember, but he overdid it at first, scanning his imaginary map in erratic desperation, sniffing in every corner at once like four hungry blind dogs, until bit by bit it began to dawn on him that a clue might be sought not only in the ghostly events of yesterday, but also in things present before him in a more homely form, and eventually his eyes fell on the airline bag at the foot of the bed.

He went and kneeled by the bag and opened the zipper. Inside he found his costume, rank with sweat, and he recalled his resolve to go to the laundromat.

In turn, the idea of the laundromat led him, sensibly, to the idea of the bicycle.

All this was promising—the idea of one object leading sensibly to the idea of another: the bag, the costume, the laundromat, the bicycle—very promising indeed. If he could keep this up, he thought, he might hold his head high and, with all confidence in a grand success, take his mind for a walk along a progression of ideas and objects, as if it were a path of cobblestones leading to the palace of wisdom.

He got to his feet, therefore, and hurried out to the front room, the livingroom, to have a look at his bicycle, which ordinarily he kept propped against the wall by the front door; the bicycle, however, was not there; only the wall was there; in consequence, he looked at the wall, not without some gratitude for its existence, and tried to imagine plausible circumstances that might have prevented him from bringing the bicycle home last night.

Perhaps the weather. Perhaps by the time he left the bar the rain had already started. In that case, however, the bicycle still might have been taken in Leskov's car. Unless Leskov had refused. But why would Leskov refuse? Out of some fastidious concern that the bicycle might damage the upholstery? This was possible, but out of character.

Perhaps, then, it had been Bennett himself who had decided to leave the bicycle in the rack. But for what reason? Laziness? Fatigue? Perhaps. Or perhaps he had passed out in the bar. In this case Leskov would have had to carry Bennett from the bar to the Buick, and then from the Buick up the walk to the apartment, and he might have felt that picking up the bicycle into the bargain was beyond the call of duty. Besides, the bicycle had been left in the rack on a lock and chain, so Leskov would have had to fish in Bennett's pockets for the key, which was on a steel ring with six other keys, and this last task might have discouraged him.

Bennett touched the outside of the trouser pocket on his right, where ordinarily he kept his keys. On confirming that his keys were where they were supposed to be, however, he was disturbed. Not by the keys. He was reassured by the keys. He was disturbed by the trousers. Not by the trousers in themselves. The trousers were brown corduroy and perfectly ordinary. He was disturbed simply by the fact that he had them on, and that also he had on his windbreaker and tennis sneakers, for this was not like him. On occasion he slept naked or in underwear, but as a rule, he slept only in pajamas. He was, in fact, inordinately partial to pajamas, and at present he owned five pair.

Since only a condition of perfect unconsciousness, in short, could have made it possible for him to go to bed in brown corduroy trousers, a windbreaker, and tennis sneakers, he thought it reasonable to suppose that he had, after all, passed out, and that he had done so, if not in the bar, then at some point located more than half a body's length from the bed; in which case, he must have been transported to the bed by at least one other person. Say, then, that the other person was Leskov. Given that the front door was of a type that could be locked from outside only with a key, and that the key was still in Bennett's pocket, it would follow that Leskov, on departing, would have had to leave the front door unlocked, and that the door should be unlocked still.

On examining the door, however, Bennett found that it was locked in two places, the lock below the doorknob and the sturdier lock above, and in addition was latched to the little chain on the inside of the doorpost.

This meant, then, either that Bennett himself had locked and chained the front door, or, in a more sinister vein, that Leskov was still in the apartment.

The apartment contained three rooms: a bedroom, a bathroom, and a livingroom that had at the rear a small kitchen in an alcove.

Bennett walked back through the bedroom and into the bathroom, which was the only room he had not been in since waking. He walked into the bathroom slowly and looked behind the door, but found nobody there. Then he drew the shower curtain, which had a shadow behind it, but he found the shadow only a shadow, a trick of the light, and nobody there either.

Whereon he remembered the closets. There were two, one in the bedroom and one in the livingroom, and he went and looked in them, but there too he found nobody, only the ordinary things. In the bedroom closet he found a few shirts, a few pairs of trousers and a gray flannel suit on wire hangers suspended from a discolored metal bar, and on the floor a laundry bag and three pairs of shoes. In the livingroom closet, he found two jackets and a coat on hangers, and on the floor a small vacuum cleaner, a broom, a pair of boots, and an umbrella.

On shutting the door of the livingroom closet, Bennett was about to give up the search, when it occurred to him that there were two more places where Leskov might hide: the oven and the refrigerator. That Leskov might hide in the oven or the refrigerator was, of course, ridiculous. Bennett saw that. He saw that clearly. Both the oven and refrigerator were too small, except for a child or a dwarf. But he went and had a look anyway, first in the oven, then the refrigerator, after which, at last, he was obliged to conclude that at present the apartment appeared to contain nobody but himself, and that he, and he alone, must have been the one who had locked and chained the door last night.

Unless, of course, Leskov had departed through the window. This, though, was implausible, because the windows were covered by screens hooked from the inside. All the same, to be certain, Bennett went and examined the windows, six in all.

Once content that all the hooks on the screens were secure, he turned his attention to the alarm clock on the night table near the bed. The time was now ten minutes to nine. He picked up the clock and examined it. The alarm bell was in the off position, and the alarm dial was at six-thirty. Six-thirty was the time he set the dial on Sunday nights to make an eight o'clock class on Monday. But today was Tuesday. And on Monday nights he reset the dial for seven-thirty, to make a nine o'clock class. Last night, however, clearly he had failed both to reset the dial and to put the bell in the on position.

In consequence, he was now too late to make the nine o'clock class, and, worse, too late to call Leskov. Ordinarily Leskov left home early and could be found by seven-thirty, having coffee in the luncheonette near campus. But perhaps today, in deference to the bad weather, he had stayed home and had coffee with his wife, and perhaps had even decided to cut class.

Bennett went to the phone in the livingroom and dialed Leskov's number. After two rings the phone was answered by Sarah, Leskov's wife. The first words that Sarah spoke were directed to her little daughter Annie, who was sobbing and whining in the background.

"Just be quiet, dear. Mommy has to talk on the phone. Oh, this child! Hello?"

"Hi, Sarah."

"David? Oh, be quiet!"

"Is Lesk . . . Is Dimitri there?"

"He just left about five minutes ago. Aren't you going to class, David?"

"No. Did he say anything about me?"

"He said you got a little drunk last night."

"Is that all?"

"What?"

"I said: Is that all he said."

"He also said that if you called, I should tell you that he'd see you after the play tonight."

"Isn't he going to be around this afternoon?"

"He's going to meet Orbach later to do some translation."

"At Orbach's place?"

"I think so. David, is something wrong?"

"I'm just nervous about the play."

"Did something happen last night between you and Dimitri?"

"Did he say something did?"

"No, but did it?"

"I'm not sure," said Bennett, after a pause.

"What? You have to talk louder, David. Annie! Please! Go and look out the window at the nice rain! What did you say, David?"

"Nothing."

"It's the thunder. The child is terrified of thunder. I don't understand. When I was a child, I always loved the thunder."

"Me too."

"What?"

"Never mind. I'll talk to you later."

"I can't hear a word you're saying, David! I'll talk to you later!"

Bennett got out of his clothes and stuffed them in a cotton bag in the bedroom closet. He took a shower, brushed his teeth and shaved, then put on fresh clothes. In a small stainless steel percolator, he made coffee, which he drank with milk and no sugar, standing by the sink. After a second cup he was ready to take his costume to the laundromat, and he called the local cab company, but the line was busy. He waited a minute, then dialed again, then again and again, but the line was continually busy, which did not surprise him. The village had only one small cab company, a filthy little storefront near the train station, and on rainy days the dispatcher usually had so many more calls than he could accommodate, that he would take the phone off the hook for long periods of time. The dispatcher was a big ox-like effeminate man with boyish little eyes, who had active class resentment against the students at the college and, apart from his routine insolence, liked to play little tricks on them, such as quoting outrageous fares, or promising to send a cab, and then never sending one. Since Bennett was in no mood for such tricks, he reflected that it might be just as well that the line was busy, and he went over to the front window to have a look at the weather and see if he might make the trip to the laundromat on foot.

The rain was still coming down hard, but the wind had let up. Lightning flashed over the rooftops in the distance. He began to count. At six, thunder struck. When it died, he went to the livingroom closet and got his raincoat and umbrella. He propped the umbrella against the wall by the front door, put on the raincoat, went and got the airline bag from the bedroom, came back through the livingroom, picked up the umbrella again, slipping it into the fist of his left hand along with the handle of the airline bag, put a ring of keys between his teeth, slipped the doorchain off the latch, unlocked the locks, twisted and pulled the doorknob, and stepped outside onto the doorstep. Hunching his shoulders against the downpour on his back, he pulled the door shut, took the ring of keys out of his teeth and locked the top lock, but not the bottom, so that on his return he would have only one lock to deal with and could get in out of the rain as quickly as possible. Then he put the keys away in a coat pocket, tucked the airline bag between his knees and, after opening the umbrella, paused abruptly, tilting his head, to look at an idea. It was an idea about the umbrella and the doorchain. The scrape and click of the umbrella, he thought, were like the scrape and click of the doorchain in the latch; moreover, it was conceivable that this likeness in the sound of the two objects was more than a nicety, in that the scrape and click may have issued not from the umbrella alone, as appearance had it, but in reality from the doorchain as well. In other words Leskov may have been in the apartment all along and, as soon as he was alone, rushed from his hiding place to the doorchain; in which case, it was likely he would now be standing not an arm's length away, one ear pressed to the inside of the door, a twinkle in his slanted eyes, smiling at his own cleverness in having slipped the chain into the latch at just the right moment to coincide with the scrape and click of the umbrella! Was this possible? Hadn't Sarah just indicated on the phone that Leskov left her only a few minutes ago?

Could she have been lying? If so, to what end? Were she and her husband collaborating in some kind of pointless mischief? Impossible. Besides, the apartment had been searched everywhere, everywhere!

Except behind the draperies that framed the living-room window. How was it that Bennett had neglected the draperies?

At once he put the key back in the lock, pushed open the door and, confirming with some relief that the chain was still, as he had left it, off the latch, he shut the umbrella and went in and had a look behind the draperies. Finding nobody there, he went and looked into everything all over again, the three rooms and two closets, and even the oven and refrigerator, proceeding on the premise that though Leskov may have been hidden originally behind the draperies, he would have had just enough time to dash over to another hiding place during the minute or so that Bennett had been outside on the doorstep.

Still finding the apartment empty, Bennett returned to the front door, ready to go out a second time, when again his attention was arrested by the door-chain, which, in spite of its static innocence, presented him with yet another question; namely, why had the chain been found on the latch in the first place? Customarily, he left the chain off the latch. In fact, he made a point every night before retiring to go and check and make sure the chain was off the latch. This nightly ritual, which was as regular a part of his routine as brushing his teeth, had been cultivated out of respect to the eccentric fear that if a fire should break out while he were asleep, a chain on the latch might fatally delay his potential rescuers. To be consistent, of course, he should also have left the locks unlocked, but somehow, the fact that the locks could be opened with a key from the outside allowed him to class them as insignificant obstacles, even though the chances that a potential rescuer would be in possession of a key were small.

This morning, in any case, he had found the chain on the latch. Of this he was certain. Why, then, had he not been alarmed at once? More significantly, if it were he who had put the chain on the latch last night, what was it that had prompted him to depart from routine to begin with? No doubt some new and urgent fear that overshadowed his customary fear that a fire might break out in his sleep. Then what was this new fear? Against what had he latched the door? Had he hurt someone from whom he anticipated reprisals? If so, then why had he left the bedroom window wide open? An enterprising pursuer in search of retribution might with the greatest of ease have ripped open the screen in one stroke. Perhaps the open window had just been a stupid oversight. Or perhaps it was the police he feared; in which case, shutting the window would have been superfluous. The police were not likely to enter through the window, or at least he would never have let matters get that far. If the police were to have come for him, he would have opened the door and faced them in good faith. That was his nature. Then why the latch? Perhaps to gain half a minute to catch his breath and ready himself? This was plausible. A delay of half a minute before the wrath of the law might appear to be as precious as life itself.

But then, what might he have done to stir up the wrath of the law?

He opened the door and went out on the doorstep. He took a deep breath of the cold air. The rain splashed his face. He tucked the umbrella under one arm and the airline bag between his knees and locked one lock. Then he opened the umbrella, took the bag by the handle, and hurried away from the house.

At the corner he turned to the left, toward the village. Bare elms and oaks lined the street on both sides. The branches of the trees on one side touched the branches of the trees on the other. Red and yellow dead leaves lay everywhere, on the road, the sidewalks, the lawns, and dammed up the drains. Again and again lightning flashed. He met no one on the way, no one on foot, though now and then a car passed. The cars had their headlights on, as if it were night. He walked on the sidewalks, as quickly as he could, but at each corner he leaped over the stream rushing along the gutter and broke into a run to cross the road.

It took him half an hour to reach the village. Once there, he kept close to the storefronts until he came to the laundromat. He peered through the glass in the door, then shut the umbrella and went inside. The shop was warm and bright. No customers were in. At the rear a radio played the news. The machines were still. He went to the rear and found the owner, sitting beside a radio no bigger than a shoebox.

Bennett asked for a cup of detergent. The owner got up and scooped some white powder from a pail into a cup.

He was a short man in his sixties. His shoulders were hunched. He was bald. One of his eyes was swollen. His hands were fat and red and freckled, the fingers rough and stubby. He wore old brown leather bedroom slippers. When he walked, he did not lift his feet, but slid one slipper after another in a weary, painful effort.

"Ten cents," he said, offering the cup with one hand and holding the other hand with palm up and the little fingers curled.

Bennett put a dime into the upturned hand and took the cup to a washer and dumped in the powder. From his airline bag he dumped his costume on top of the powder, then shut the lid and put a quarter in the slot. The washer began to rumble.

"You'll catch pneumonia."

This was said by the old man, whose approach had escaped Bennett's notice.

"Take off your sneakers and socks and put them in the drier," continued the old man. "Also the pants. You're soaked up to the knees."

"I can't walk around here in my underwear," said Bennett.

"I got a pair of pants that maybe will fit you."

The old man went and brought out a pair of large overalls from the lost-and-found bin. Bennett got out of his sneakers and socks and put them in a drier. Then he emptied his trouser pockets and put his trousers in as well. While he was getting into the overalls, he saw the old man stand up on his toes and put a dime in the drier.

"You don't have to do that," said Bennett.

26

The old man shrugged his shoulders and walked back to the radio and sat down.

After a pause Bennett went and also sat by the radio.

"If you are going to sit here, don't talk," said the old man.

The two men sat in brown bridge chairs with metal frames and plastic seats. Bennett put his elbows on his knees, his wrists limp, the fingers of his left hand curled loosely around his right thumb, and bowed his head, cocking it in the direction of the radio, which repeatedly emitted bursts of static caused by the storm, while a solemn nasal voice, accompanied by the tapping of a tickertape, delivered international news—ministers and kings, and rebels in the hills—like odd bits and pieces of a shattered romance.

Why, wondered Bennett, had the old man been so nice? He was not a nice man. He was a mean man, a spiteful man; no doubt his liver was diseased. He had the only laundromat in town, and he ran it like a bureau in hell. He pinched the ladies when they bent over their bags. When a washer broke down, he cried mischief and threatened to sue. When a washer was overloaded, he grabbed a fistful of the excess and flung it on the floor. When customers came in near six o'clock, which was closing time, he sold them soap and made change and watched like a witch at a brew as the laundry was loaded in the washers, and then, promptly at six, he switched off the lights without warning and told everyone to get out and either leave the laundry overnight or take it home wet. He seldom cleaned the filters or the drains, and the laundry always came out adorned with lint and hair and all sorts of disgusting alien particles. In every respect he was a penance. Yet this morning he had been nice, nice to Bennett. Why? Why me? thought Bennett. There was no telling, no telling. It was a mystery. Like the chain on the door.

The local news came on. Dust and discretion. Zones. Funds. Boards and bureaus. Crime was the one crested wave on the air. Last night the county had one arson, one rape, one murder, and one assault with a knife. Each was less than an hour away by car, and Bennett surmised he could have done them all. He could have burned the barbershop in North Branch, raped the highschool girl in Loomis, shot the accountant in Parksville, and stabbed the trucker in Cahoonzie, and still got home before dawn.

When the laundry was done, he folded the costume and put it carefully into the airline bag; then he got into his trousers and sneakers and socks and returned the overalls to the old man and thanked him. The old man did not look up. He sat and listened to the news, gazing at the floor, and carelessly tossed the overalls over his shoulder back into the bin from which they came. The news items had already been repeated three or four times—the same ministers, the same kings, the same rebels in the hills, the same funds and boards and bureaus, the same fire, the same rape, the same murder, the same assault with a knife— but still the old man listened, waiting perhaps for some new development.

Bennett left the shop. The storm had let up. There was no wind to speak of, and the rain had subsided

28

to a fine misty drizzle. He hurried through the streets, hoping to get back home before the storm started up again. On the way he contemplated crime, not only the felonious aberrations reported on the news, but other crimes, crimes of the spirit and crimes of the soul, sordid unspeakable crimes, and the sly dark acts of the pretty and the shy. He supposed that if he could picture enough crimes vividly enough, eventually one of them would tap the vault of forgetfulness, and then the memory of the crime he had actually committed last night would return like a prodigal son. But his mind kept wandering, drifting nonsensically into regions of the ordinary—a paper that was due in a course on the nineteenth-century European novel, the pale strong legs of a young woman he had passed among the bookshelves in the library two days ago—distracting him from his deeper purpose.

As soon as he got home, he called Orbach's number, in the hope that Leskov would be there. But no one answered. He paced around the apartment for a few minutes. He tried to concentrate on crime. The images were pale, confused. Try as he might, he could not pursue any of the imaginary scenes to the end, and the exercise began to bore and weary him.

He went to the bookcase near the foot of his bed and ran his eyes along the titles on the spines. The bookcase was made of unfinished pine, with five shelves, about four feet across, stacked tightly with paperback books from Penguin and Modern Library and Grosset & Dunlap, all of which had been read by him within the last year, each in either one or two sittings. Sometimes he would begin a book at breakfast and read until midnight, keeping his eyes fixed on the page, even when he got up to relieve himself or to make a pot of coffee or a sandwich. All the books, except the tales of Edgar Allen Poe and a collection of the short late works of Herman Melville, were by European authors, and all were preoccupied with the dark and sinister side of life. Some of them so intrigued and astonished him that he bought duplicate copies and sent them off as gifts. Such gifts he sent not on birthdays or holidays but just as the fancy took him and with feverish indiscretion. To his mother he sent a short novel in which a middle-aged clerk, who sees himself as an enemy of the type of the Rational Man, tortures a young consumptive prostitute. To his father he sent a long novel in which a university student, on the principle that he is a superior individual and beyond the law, murders an old woman with an axe. To his closest cousin, a frail, timid woman, now a sophomore at a women's college in Vermont, he sent a philosophic poem in which the author proclaims in thunderous rhythms the death of God and scorns the merciful postures of the Christ. In response, Bennett received no thank-you notes, only long distance calls of concern. To this concern he replied with reassurances, that he was perfectly all right, that the books were just books, that they had nothing to do with him, and that he was the same David Bennett he had always been. But this was not so. The books that he sent, and the others like them, coincided with a sharp turn in the current of his disposition, and, under their spell, he was mortified by his own innocence, convinced that his youth had been misspent in a cloud of vapid illusion, and that the code of virtue he had tried to live up to for so long was an impudent litany designed to humiliate and confine him.

In one of these books, he thought, squatting to peer at the titles on the bottom shelf, he might find a clue to the mystery of last night. But which book? There were so many, so many. Moreover, his legs had begun to ache, and he was tired. Why was he so tired? What time had he got home last night? Pushing both hands down on his knees, he straightened up with a sigh; then he went to the bathroom sink and splashed cold water in his face, but the water did little to revive him, and he allowed that it really might be best to lie down for a while. So he went and sat on the edge of the bed and took off his shoes and lay down. He lay down on his back with his hands behind his head. A ten- or fifteen-minute nap, he decided, would do him a world of good. And then, refreshed, he could go and spend an hour or so at his desk, writing in his journal, and maybe the stern labor of pressing a ballpoint pen on a pad of paper would induce his mind to open its doors.

When he awoke, he woke with a start and glanced at the clock on the night table. Seeing that it was nearly six o'clock, he leaped out of bed, cursing aloud. He was due at the theater at six-thirty, and the walk ordinarily took about forty-five minutes. The play was scheduled to begin at eight. He hurried into the bathroom and brushed his teeth and ran a comb through his hair; then he returned to the bedroom and got into his jacket and shoes and picked up the airline bag and rushed over to look out the window in the front room. The rain had stopped altogether. There was no wind. It was dark. The street lamps were on. The road glistened. The moon shone on the puddles in the gutters. He went out the door without an umbrella, dismissing it as an unnecessary precaution. After a brief pause on the doorstep, he decided to leave the door unlocked. He had a reason for this. He was certain he had a reason. Nevertheless he could not have said what it was, and he did not linger over it, but set off resolutely, not entirely without some misgivings about the unlocked door and the mysterious nature of his own reasons, and then he hurried away from the house.

He wore no watch, so he did not know the time when he arrived at the theater. The lights were on in the lobby. Three cars were parked out front by the curb. He recognized them. They belonged to members of the cast. Though he had run a good part of the way, he concluded that he was late, and he dreaded the censure that awaited him inside.

In a bicycle rack near the curb, beyond the pale light of the street lamp, stood five bicycles in silhouette. One of them, the one on the far left, he assumed was his; but when he moved closer, he found it to be another bicycle altogether—a green racer that belonged to the assistant director. On the ground a few feet to the right of the green racer lay a broken chain. Bennett squatted and picked the chain up and examined it. It had been cut, apparently with heavy shears. The ends were clean and sharp and glistened. Recognizing the broken chain as his own, he inferred that he must now be discovering it a second time. The first time, likely, was at some point in the previous night, and that is why he had come home without the bicycle. This was a simple, obvious inference, and as it settled the bicycle question neatly, he walked away from the rack with a smile, somewhat lighter of heart, reflecting that under ordinary circumstances, the discovery that his bicycle had been stolen would have marked the beginning, not the end, of a mystery.

The clock in the lobby read six-forty. He was only ten minutes late. He went into the theater, down the aisle, then up across the stage, through the wings and back along the corridor to the dressing room. It was a large room, with many small mirrors. The whole cast of fifteen actors was assembled in it. At the door he was greeted by Dicataldo with an affectionate embrace. Surprised and grateful, Bennett blushed, then went in and began to prepare for the play.

He took his time. He got out of his ordinary clothes, folded them neatly, and laid them on a chair. Then he went and stood before a mirror to put on his costume. It was a simple costume, a flannel shirt, faded blue jeans, and brown work boots. He wore the shirtsleeves rolled up on the forearms, and the jeans cuffed. He put pancake makeup on his face, darkened his eyebrows, and pasted on the beard. All this he did very slowly. Now and then he exchanged a few words with the other actors, whose general mood was one of repressed excitement.

At about half past seven, while brooding over a line in the raindrop speech, he was tapped on the shoulder by the stage manager, a thin attractive woman, who put her mouth close to his ear and whispered that "some people" were asking to see him in the corridor. With apprehension, he laid the script on the table and went to the door. The corridor was dimly lit, but he had no trouble in recognizing his visitors at once. They were his mother and father, Susan and Jack Bennett. He moved them away from the door, out of sight of the cast.

"We won't keep you," Susan Bennett said. "We just wanted to wish you luck." And Jack Bennett said, with a guarded smile, "You look good in a beard."

Then they stood in silence for a moment and glowed. They glowed like supernatural beings, scented and splendidly arrayed. From Susan came the scent of lilac, from Jack menthol and wintergreen and peppermint. Susan wore a shiny fur coat with long hairs. She wore silver earrings decked with rhinestones, and a matching necklace and bracelet. She wore gray shoes and a pale lavender dress trimmed with gray lace. She wore mascara on her eyelashes and blue shadow under her eyes. Her lips and fingernails were painted a soft pink. Jack wore a dark blue suit and a dark blue tie handpainted with tiny roses, and a starched shirt with blue and white stripes. He wore gold cufflinks and a gold tiepin. His shoes were black and shone like glass. Over one arm he held a beige woolen overcoat with leather buttons and a beige hat with a feather in the band.

Both parents were handsome and youthful. Jack was a little over fifty, Susan a little under. Jack was dark, Susan fair. Their backs were straight, and their movements were in perfect accord, as though choreo-

34

graphed in eternity. Their voices were moderate, and their English bore no trace of a regional accent. They had no eccentric gestures, not a blemish on the skin, and they gave off an air of being engaged in a tender romance of impeccable standards.

The last time they had visited their son was one Sunday afternoon about a month ago, toward the end of October, five or six days after they had telephoned to express concern over the dark European novels he had sent. They turned up on his doorstep out of the blue, without phoning beforehand, dressed with the same fresh elegance with which they were dressed tonight, and explained that they had been out for a drive, were just passing by, and thought they would drop in and say hello. Bennett had been reading a novel for six hours, and he had not shaved in four days; there were a pile of unwashed dishes in the sink and papers strewn on the floor. As soon as his mother stepped into the apartment, a tear formed in her eye. The father only smiled, seemed a little embarrassed, and scarcely said a word during the entire visit. The son offered to make coffee, but the mother said they had just had coffee at a Howard Johnson's. No mention was made of the dark European novels, except by way of a subtle allusion, when she recommended a very witty, very sane, very healthy book she had just read, a book by a man named Harry Golden. Bennett said that he had never heard of Harry Golden or the book, but would certainly look it up. There was no need, she said, for she would send him a copy. Then, though not five minutes had passed since her

35

arrival, she rose abruptly from the sofa and said to the father that they ought to be getting home. The son was astonished and bewildered. At the door she lingered for a moment to kiss him on the cheek, adding in a gentle whisper that, really, he ought to shave, because a clean appearance always lifted the spirits; then she stepped outside and hurried down the path after the father, her head bowed, her shoulders shaking, as if she were crying.

The brief visit upset Bennett deeply. He did not believe that his parents had been just passing by. This was absurd. The college was several hundred miles from home, and he could not imagine any reason for their driving to this area. On the other hand, if they had driven all this way just to see him, why had they stayed less than five minutes?

Two hours after they left, while he was standing by the stove and putting up a pot of coffee, he had a fleeting vision of them in their Pontiac crossing the Tappenzee Bridge. He could see the bridge clearly. The sun was setting. The car was moving rather slowly in heavy traffic, and they were engaged in a painful argument, shouting at each other angrily.

This vision, in its luminous clarity, had the aspect of a real event, though in fact, in all the years he had lived with them, he had never witnessed such an argument, had never even once heard them raise their voices against each other in anger. At about eight p.m., which was the time he estimated they would be getting home, he contemplated phoning to ask if they actually had such an argument on the Tappenzee Bridge, but he restrained himself, judging that a call of this kind would only disconcert them further and do him no good in their eyes.

That night he had a restless sleep, which concluded with a dream about a woman who stood between two paths at the edge of a dark forest. The woman looked something like his mother, but was taller and younger, and wore a long flowing white gown. She beckoned him and, indicating the path on the right, said that this was the path of honor. As he took her outstretched hand, suddenly she grasped him tightly, transformed into a hideous witch, and drew him to the other path, the path on the left, whispering with perverse delight that this was the path of shame, at which point she vanished, and an invisible force began to draw him into the path. Ahead he saw ominous shadows. He tried to go back, but the invisible force kept drawing him in, deeper and deeper, until, overwhelmed by terror, he woke up in a sweat with a stifled cry in his throat at about five a.m.

He got up and went out to the kitchen to make coffee. Brooding on the dream, he was unable to make head or tail of it, except that he supposed it must have had something to do with the visit from his parents the previous day.

Jack and Susan Bennett owned a brick house in a prim suburban town on the south shore of Long Island, and they both worked.

Susan worked as a clerk in a large department store. The store paid her a small salary plus a commission on sales. Her department was Furniture For Infants. She had worked in that department from the outset nine years ago, and she had steadfastly refused all opportunities to transfer to other departments. She had also refused promotions to manager or to buyer. She did not want to manage or to buy. She wanted to sell. She wanted to sell furniture to infants. Infants, she observed, had optimistic taste, were indiscriminate with the dollar, and in general did most of their shopping before they were born, so that more often than not she found herself transacting business with a transcendent clientele, radiant and potent and unimaginably harmonious, as if the very forms of a most substantial heaven had come to her, and her alone, for good advice and nurture. On the surface things may have looked otherwise, but at bottom her grander view was more to the point. The weary caravans of mordant, swollen mothers and anxious fathers were not, in essential fact, the real customers on the floor. They were mere agents in the ineluctable service of a better class.

Jack too was in sales. But he was not a retail clerk. He was wholesale and freelance, and he traveled. He traveled Long Island, New Jersey and upstate New York. He traveled Connecticut and a few towns in Pennsylvania. He sold Sportswear for Ladies—long pants and short pants and pedal-pushers, blouses and shirts, jackets and sweaters, slick plastic belts, and cashmere berets in five colors. The buyers were all ladies, and he took pride in the seductive delicacy of his pitch. Often he told stories about the competition, genial stories, in which all his rivals were brash and pushy and consequently not so successful as he. He crossed their paths in the shops, the motels, and the diners. At night they drank and smoked and cheated on their wives. But not he. At night Jack liked to eat something light and take a shower and read a few pages of a book and go to sleep before nine. For these mild habits his rivals admired and respected him. The rivals admired and respected him, and the buyers were in love with him. This was his view of the matter. And it was a grand, even a noble view. Mounted on the seat of the latest Pontiac, armored in iron and steel and chromium plate, he was a sage and tender mercantile knight, pure as the snow through which he had driven thirteen winters, his virtue shining like headlights on dark and twilit roads.

But he had not always been this. Previously, from 1938 to 1946, he worked as a machinist in a factory that made airplane parts. He ground and shaped steel. He wore helmets and dark glasses to shield him from the dust of the metal and the poisonous light. His hands were bruised and calloused. He sweated. He ached. He worked overtime at time-and-a-half. He worked in an attitude of contained frenzy, with furrowed brow and a keen malicious eye, amid the brassy percussive voices of a thousand machines and the scatalogical epithets of the other workers, the grim abusive commands of the foreman. He wore blue shirts and carried a black lunchpail with a thermos in it. In the thermos was black coffee with no sugar. His food he wrapped in wax paper, usually a sandwich of cold lima beans and a slice of raw onion. In those days he wished to disengage from the current collective cruelty to animals, and he ate no meat, but he could not disengage from cruelty itself, so he turned it away from animals and onto the raw lining of his own mouth and tongue and throat and stomach. The onion was not good if it did not burn. He liked Mexican peppers. He liked thick coffee one day old. He liked coarse salt, which he ate by the ounce out of his hand. He liked burnt toast and stale bread and the shells of hardboiled eggs. In these esoteric practices he persisted day in and day out for years on end, earning a reputation at the plant as a machinist of stone character and an authentic eater of difficult things—until one day in the spring of 1946, about half an hour before the lunch whistle, while standing at a lathe and honing the head of a piston, he took off his helmet, turned in response to a familiar sardonic voice, and broke his foreman's jaw with one swift right hook that had been premeditated for eight years but nevertheless took everyone by surprise, and he was fired on the spot. Two weeks later he collapsed at the end of a line in the unemployment bureau and was rushed by ambulance to a hospital, where two feet of his intestinal tract and half his stomach were cut out as a stay against impish ulceration and a mad acidic tide. After this, convalescing in the hospital for two weeks, he took up a bland diet. Noodles and cottage cheese and warm milk. Farina and boiled rice and melba toast. Poached eggs and steamed halibut and now and then a bit of ground beef. He ate only small amounts, but he ate eight times a day. Nothing fried, nothing raw, no salt, no pepper, no garlic. Also he read. He read *How to Win Friends and Influence People* by Dale Carnegie, and *The Power of Positive Thinking* by Norman Vincent Peale. He read *Ecclesiastes* in a

Gideon bible. He read them again and again, Carnegie and Peale and the prophet of *Ecclesiastes,* and out of the print, line by line, he bred a smile tempered by resignation. On the last day, from his roommate's wife, he got a thin magazine that ran ads seeking salesmen for manufacturers of ladies' clothes. With this magazine, along with the new diet, the new books, and the new smile, he stepped out of the hospital a new man, baptized in lukewarm waters, an acolyte of peace and conciliation, and he prospered—cultivating day by day, amid the winds of fortune and adversity, a mode of action that would stand as a reproach against the agencies of evil, never considering that the agencies of evil, by their very nature, and unlike the agencies of good, were irreproachable.

There was one more thing he got in the hospital. From a book of Inspirational Quotations, he got a line about the mean, misquoted from Aristotle. In the original text, Aristotle elaborated the meaning of the mean with the metaphor of the eye in the target of an archer. But Jack Bennett had not been graced with the original text. He had only the Inspirational Anthology, and so he came up with a metaphor of his own, which was not the eye in the target of an archer, but the middle of the road of a quietist. Whenever he spoke of the mean, he spoke of it not plainly as the mean, as had Aristotle, but as The Golden Mean, as had the Inspirational Anthology, and he embraced it not as a mere guiding principle, but as something much, much higher, as a shimmering cosmic totem, perfect and absolute, with which he might replace completely and for all time the fierce demanding God that he had worshipped as a ritualistic Jew in childhood and tried to eat alive in the painful revolt of manhood—the Unnamed Wrathful Jealous God, the Manic-Depressive Father in the Sky, of Moses, of Abraham and Isaac and Jesus, and of all the generations of Jews for five millenia.

As for Susan Bennett, she also was a Jew, but she had never been ritualistic, even as a child. She was a woman of transcendent design and would rather have been a totem herself than a worshipper of one. Nevertheless, her husband was her husband, his mean was her mean, and whither he went, she watched.

Tonight, on this cold November night in 1959, in the dim backstage corridor, Susan and Jack Bennett stood in clear relief against old unadorned walls, radiating the tender will of good gods, until, suddenly, there appeared at their backs a pair of phantoms. To the son the phantoms were like versions of the parents, but younger and grimmer. The phantom mother held a washboard, the father a black lunchbox. Then a second pair of phantoms appeared. This pair were quite sinister. Their mouths were twisted in a hideous conspiratorial grin. Their eyes were orange and flickered with mischief and malice. They had daggers in their belts and bright bandanas around their necks. Their lips were blue, their teeth white as ivory. The phantoms in fact were student actors, running through the corridor on their way from the dressing room to the wings to arrange the props. But as they passed, for the moment they appeared to be participating as figures in a revelatory vision. And so potent, so rich, so complex was this fleeting spontaneous pantomime in the corridor, that the son wished he could have meditated on it in motionless ecstacy for a long time, inviting his parents to meditate along with him, so that at the end all three, father, mother, and son, might have a wonderful speculative conversation and plumb the depths and discover and create substance and ornament out of the abysmal fabric of their destiny. But as it stood, he had other pressing matters to attend to. He needed to return to the dressing room and get the props he would carry in his pocket on-stage—the dagger, the silver dollar, and the deck of cards. He needed to do his breathing exercises and look over the lines of the raindrop speech again. He needed to wish the other actors luck and touch each one with his hands. And most of all, he needed to empty his mind of all things outside the province of the play. So, he hastily bid his mother and his father goodbye and, with their good wishes fluttering behind him like pigeons in pursuit, hurried back into the dressing room and shut the door.

"Was that your parents?" said Dicataldo.

"No, no, just people from the neighborhood," said Bennett. "My parents couldn't come."

And at once he went to the mirror across the room and had a second look at his makeup. Why he had lied about his parents he had no idea. The lie had come to him on the spur of the moment. He knew only that if his actual parents had resembled either of the phantom couples that had fled through the corridor a moment ago, no such lie would have occurred to him. On the contrary, he would have ushered them into the dressing room without hesitation and, with dark pride in his origins, made a show of them to the company.

The play ran two-and-a-half hours through twenty-eight scenes and had thirty-seven characters. There were only fifteen actors, and most of them played at least two parts. Karl Greenfield was the title character, and he was played by Bennett. The place was North Dakota, the time 1843. Why North Dakota, and why 1843, Bennett had no idea. He knew nothing about North Dakota beyond its position on the map, and nothing about the situation in 1843. For him, North Dakota signified the remote and the arid, the land of rock and sand, whirlwind and dust, deadly sun and deadly night, violent eruptions and torrential rain, feast and famine, serpents and sheep and sacred minerals in subterranean promise—the Middle East of the Northwest.

Out of this place rose the hero, Karl Greenfield, a potent saturnine man, for whom all the other characters, as well as the land itself, comprised the articulated components of a single tortuous problem, which, though it compelled his every move, he could not name.

Karl lived with his family on a farm. They kept sheep and chickens and some goats. The main crops were wheat and corn. The family was large: Karl, his mother and elder brother, an aunt, an uncle, two young nephews, and the mother's parents. The father was dead, and Karl and his elder brother were the heads of the household.

The elder brother was gentle and otherworldly. He had lucid, prophetic visions. He was chaste and still unmarried at the age of thirty. He had developed a reputation as a seer and a healer and a wise counselor among the family and a few people from the neighboring farms and villages. What religious tradition he came out of was not specified in the text, and this ambiguity, along with the quaint metaphysical mode of his speech, lent him the air of an allegorical disembodied character.

Under his guidance the family prospered. The crops were abundant, the land rich and ingeniously irrigated. They produced so much and their profits were so big that they were able to accumulate vast stores of grain and enough capital to ensure their well-being for many years.

The play opens in the midst of a drought. The neighboring farmers are in trouble, and food is scarce. The Greenfields announce that they will give grain to all who are hungry. From miles around, villagers and farmers, in wagons, on horseback, and on foot, come to the Greenfield farm to apply for the promised grain, and they all go away with enough to get through two or three months.

A conflict arises between the two brothers. Karl maintains that the generosity of the family, under the guidance of the elder brother, is indiscriminate and dangerous. To this the elder brother replies with a pious rebuke, and the rest of the family support him.

Eventually the mayor turns up. With him are the sheriff, two deputies, and a posse of civilians. The mayor, portrayed in caricature as a fat, stupid, greedy lecher with a booming voice, announces that he intends to confiscate the Greenfield grain, and that he has a legal right to do so as an emergency measure for the public welfare. The elder brother submits with a sullen passivity, but Karl speaks up, protesting that the grain has been offered to all who want it, and that there is no need for the law to intervene and exact by force what has already been offered freely and with no thought of gain.

Though Karl argues reasonably and with feeling, the mayor sweeps him aside with a satiric remark and, turning to the sheriff, says that all that needed to be said has been said, and that it is now time to go to the barn and start loading the grain in the wagons. As the sheriff and the deputies and posse leave the house, Karl follows. In the barn he gives in to a fit of rage, shouting and cursing and grabbing the sacks of grain from the hands of first this one, then that one, until at last an attempt to restrain him is made by the sheriff and the two deputies. In the ensuing struggle, Karl hits the sheriff in the ribs, pushing him to the ground, and in the end kills him by kicking his head against a castiron wagonwheel propped against the wall.

At last restrained by the posse, Karl is bound hand and foot and taken back to the courthouse in the village, where he is given a perfunctory trial before the local judge and sentenced to hang three days hence at six o'clock in the morning.

While awaiting execution, he has three important visitors in his jail cell.

The first is a young woman. Her name is Anna. Anna is fair and tender and distressed, and she loves

46

him. Also he loves her. They had planned to marry in the coming spring. He tells her to have heart. He will escape, he says, and then the two of them will run off to Canada and start a new life. He tells her to meet him in a certain secluded clearing in the pine forest where they have met many times before. She is to meet him on the night of the day appointed for his execution, which, he assures her, will never take place. Meanwhile, she must not breathe a word of his plan to escape, not even to his family, who, he adds, have a peculiar commitment to the practice of honest speech, which could ruin him.

The second visitor is the jailer. The jailer is a thin devious man who talks through his nose and walks with a limp. After a brief comic negotiation, he accepts the promise of a bribe of one thousand dollars, to be deposited under a certain rock at the southeast corner of a certain abandoned windmill at the edge of the village, on condition that he leave the cell door unlocked on the morning of the execution.

On that morning the third visitor appears. It is the elder brother. In his customary style he delivers a long ornate speech, in which he takes on himself the responsibility for the tragic murder in the barn. The lighting is dim and so arranged as to suggest a shaft of early morning light coming in through a barred window. As he speaks, he paces back and forth, passing in and out of the shaft of light. He too, he says, ought to have raised his voice against the mayor and protested the expropriation of the grain. He sees that now. He has been too meek. His generosity has been indiscriminate. Further, the prosperity of the farm is the result of ten years' labor, in which he took too small a part, so preoccupied has he been with his meditations and the affairs of his neighbors, all of whom now will surely, and with just cause, reproach him with the neglect of his own house. Whether they reproach him aloud, or in their hearts, is beside the point. The principal thing is that they will reproach him. A shadow has been cast over his authority, and they will withdraw their trust and affection. This humiliation, of course, may lead him to a higher wisdom. But what does he want with a higher wisdom?

"The truth is," he says, "it is I who should go to the gallows! If I had been more attentive to your words, you would not be facing this dawn of terror and ignominy! Can you ever find it in your heart to forgive me?"

With his back to the elder brother, Karl replies, "Though I do not count myself as the occupant of an office of such a height that I have authority to administer forgiveness, if I did occupy such an office, I would surely forgive you, and with all my heart."

"Thank you, Karl," says the elder brother, and then he steps a little closer, takes a thick wooden club from inside his coat, strikes Karl on the back of the head, knocking him unconscious, and drags him across the cell and hides him under the bed.

When the jailer returns, he says, "Where's your brother?" And the elder brother, now lying on his side on top of the bed, his face turned to the wall, answers in a muffled voice, "He left."

With this, the scene ends. The stage is dark for a few moments. Then the lights come up again, to reveal

Karl stirring under the bed. He crawls out in a daze, rubbing the back of his head, and goes to the window, through which he sees the lifeless form of the elder brother hanging on the gallows.

At once Karl delivers a soliloquy, condemning both the arrogance of his brother's futile sacrifice, and his own failure to anticipate and forestall it, and then he puts on a jacket and slips out of the cell, and the lights go down.

How the elder brother managed to bring off his valiant imposture, deceiving not only the jailer, the hangman, the mayor, and other officials of the law, but also the crowd of idle spectators and the entire family of Greenfields, is never questioned, neither by Karl, nor any other character in the play.

When the lights come up, Karl is with Anna, who informs him that the imposture has been discovered, that a search party is looking for him, that his family is in a state of inconsolable grief, and that now not only the stores of grain, but also the entire Greenfield property, have been expropriated by the mayor.

Karl and Anna stand on opposite sides of the stage. Each one is in a separate pool of light that comes from an overhead pinspot. The rest of the stage is dark. Though the lovers in reality are supposed to be standing face to face, in actual fact on the stage they are separated by about twenty or twenty-five yards, and are looking out into the audience, or, rather, above the audience, into dark, empty space.

Karl tells Anna that he wants her to care for his family. He wants her to take them to her home, where she lives alone with her parents. He has brought with him a sum of money that should be enough to provide for both families for one year, after which time, and precisely on the same day of the month, he will return. He will return, and he will meet Anna in this very place in which they now stand, and then they will marry and go off, as they had intended previously, to Canada, and start a new life. Meanwhile, he must make his escape from the county and try and get enough money to provide a decent life for his mother and grandparents and aunt and uncle and two nephews, and for Anna and himself, enough to buy land in Canada for all of them. When Anna asks how he intends to get so much money in so short a time, he tells her to have faith, and then he begins to talk about the raindrops on the trees. This is the first time trees and raindrops have been mentioned, and suddenly it is clear that the two lovers are not afloat in pools of light in dark vacuity, but are standing in a forest, in which the trees are still wet from a rain that had apparently been both heavy and recent, for large raindrops, according to the lovers, are visibly clinging to the boughs.

How the lovers have managed to remain dry and well groomed amid the recent downpour is unstated. Perhaps each traveled by way of covered wagon, or perhaps they had umbrellas. In any event, in light of Karl's rhapsodic disseration on the raindrop as an analogue of the world, covered wagons and umbrellas are of small account.

Ultimately, the raindrop theme transforms into a new theme, that of eternal love, and then, more specifically, Karl's own personal eternal love for Anna.

In response, Anna too takes up the raindrop theme, and though it had seemed that all possible variations had been exhausted by Karl, she comes up with new ones. At the last, she too declares eternal love and, in a surprising move, steps out of her pool of light, crosses the dark stage, and steps into the pool of light occupied by Karl, whereon the two lovers embrace, and the lights fade.

The next scene introduces a fantastic character, a spry old man with twinkling eyes, who represents Time, and is played by the same actor who played the jailer. Time sits cross-legged at the start of Karl's journey and speaks in rhymes and puns and alliterative phrases. His message is, on the one hand, cautionary, and on the other, an invitation to mischief. In conclusion, he wishes Karl good luck, warns him to keep his promise to return punctually one year from today, and then, as the lights fade, cries, "Farewell!" adding a series of words that likewise end in "ell" and, like the reverberations of a bell, fall off in diminuendo.

The one-year journey is depicted in a pantomime accompanied by music. Karl moves stealthily through a series of spotlights, and in each one he commits a robbery, now with a dagger, now with a pistol, now with bare hands, against various figures in silhouette. Over his shoulder he carries a red sack.

At the end he meets Time again. Time sits in the same attitude as before, but on the opposite side of the stage. Though he still talks in rhymes and puns and alliterative phrases, now his tone is ominous, for Karl has miscalculated the year, alas, and has returned one day late.

51

With foreboding, he rushes off to the forest to meet Anna. It is night. The moon is a thin crescent. He finds the limp body of Anna, a noose around her neck, hanging from a bough of the very same tree that only one year ago had provided, along with a complement of raindrops, a fertile theme for rhapsodic invention. The body hangs in silhouette against the sky. A crowd is gathered. Karl takes someone aside from the edge of the crowd.

The someone is his aunt. The aunt tells him that Anna had come to the forest the night before, expecting to meet him and was met instead by the mayor, who had been making advances to her all year, and finally, in this secluded place, raped her and then ran away, after which Anna, in despair and insupportable rage, believing into the bargain that she had been forsaken by Karl, hanged herself from the tree.

How Anna managed to do this ingenious thing, and by what agency the aunt learned what she has just reported, are unstated.

At once Karl steps into the crowd, finds the mayor, takes out a dagger, and stabs him to death under the ribs and flees.

The lights go down and then come up on a crowded saloon. Karl sits alone at a table downstage. He is drunk. On the table are a bottle of whiskey and a glass. The other patrons, located upstage, are indulging in noisy conversation about the murder of the mayor, the suicide of Anna, the barren farms, the inflated economy, and the dissolution of things in general.

Suddenly a young man enters and in great agitation announces that the village is burning. The patrons rush to the window to have a look. Another young man enters. He shouts, "It's the Greenfields! The Greenfields are burning the village!" Karl is stirred by this. He leaps out of his chair and runs out the door. He surveys the fiery rooftops and, with ecstatic jubilation, praises in soliloquy this long overdue revolt of the Greenfields. Then he picks up a burning brand and, raising it in defiance, runs off to join his family in the flames of insurrection.

The lights go down and come up.

Karl enters a prison cell, in which the rest of the Greenfields are sitting morosely on benches. Karl is feverish and triumphant. His face is streaked with cinderdust. He rushes from one Greenfield to the next, embracing each one, and praises them all maniacally. He is so proud of them, so proud! But they hang their heads and avoid his eyes. When he quiets down, sobered by the discomfort in the faces around him, the family tells him they had nothing to do with the fire. They have been used as scapegoats, they say; the village was burned in fact not by them, but by local businessmen for the insurance benefits.

Aside to the audience, Karl speaks of his disappointment in finding that his family have not burned the village, after all, that they are the same as ever, sheepish dreamers, committed to their innocence. As for himself, he concludes in despair, he is no better than they. Everyone in the village saw him running through the streets with a burning brand and heard him shouting, "This is fire from the Greenfields! Fire from the Greenfields!" and as a result, the whole family are certain to be convicted of arson and hanged. In short, he who had sought to exalt them has, in the last analysis, only paved the way to their untimely death in humiliating circumstances.

In the next scene the Greenfields stand before the gallows, awaiting execution. Karl is the first to have a noose put around his neck. He speaks a few words of quiet resignation, and the lights fade, then come up on a brief scene in which anonymous characters discuss with dispassion and irony the fate of the Greenfields and the future of the village, and the final curtain falls.

After the small generous audience had demanded and received three curtain calls, Bennett hurried off through the wings in high spirits, wishing that the stage were the world, the only world, and that he could step at once into another play, then another, and another, forever and ever.

In the corridor backstage he accepted congratulations from his parents, who were the first visitors to appear.

Embracing him, both marvelled effusively at what they had just seen on the stage, and then the mother informed him that he was trembling from head to foot and was drenched, absolutely drenched, in sweat.

"Where do you get all that energy?" said the father with a smile.

By way of a reply, Bennett laughed nervously.

As he laughed, his parents exchanged a look. It was a conspiratorial look, and it unnerved him. His heart began to race, and his laugh, which had been false to begin with, caught in his throat. To hide his confusion, he excused himself awkwardly and hurried over to the fountain in an alcove nearby and, with his back to his parents, stooped over and took a long drink of water. When he drank his fill, he cupped one hand by the spout and splashed water on his forehead and his eyelids, and then he took another long drink. He kept doing this, over and over, now splashing, now drinking, giving himself time to calm down before facing his parents again.

Certainly there had been other times when such unnerving looks had been exchanged by them in his presence, dark looks of darker implication, suggesting that they knew something, something specifically relating to him, of which they could not speak, but on the present occasion the look had a specially sinister cast, and he supposed that the something in question must be something about last night, and about what he had done. Since last night they were two hundred miles away in Long Island, however, it was unlikely they could know what he had done unless someone had phoned and told them; but as no acquaintance of his on campus knew them or had their number, the one person who might plausibly have phoned them was himself. Perhaps that was it then. He himself had phoned them. He had phoned last night, confessed to some crime, and then into the bargain persuaded them to vow never to speak of it again. That would explain everything. It would explain how they knew, why they did not speak, and the meaning of the dark look, and it would explain it all very neatly. It would even explain their peculiar response to his play. The truth was that he had been suspicious of their response as soon as they gave it. In their effusions he had detected a note of revulsion and mockery, which had initially puzzled and distressed him, but now, on reconsideration, seemed quite understandable, given that they were obliged to view the play under the aspect of some sordid crime he had confessed to them only the night before. After all, in the play he had played the part of a criminal who did things that might be no worse than what they knew him to have done in actual fact, and as they were such gentle people, so good and kind and moderate, it was only to be expected that a host of hostile alien ironies would have passed through their minds as they sat in the theater assessing this play of his that he loved.

When Bennett was calm enough to face his parents, he left the fountain and started to approach them, trying to frame in his mind a question, a leading, matter-of-fact question, which, while avoiding any reference to amnesia, might elicit some information about what they knew or did not know about last night; but just then, Leskov appeared in the lighted doorway at the far end of the passage, and Bennett put his question aside and quickened his pace.

Placing his arms around the shoulders of both his parents, he told them hastily that he was very sorry, that he would like to spend more time with them, but that he was expected by the director and the cast and the crew immediately, and that he would then have to go and help them prepare the refreshments for a party that was restricted to students.

Susan Bennett, though clearly put off by this abrupt announcement, said that of course she understood, and that he ought to attend to whatever he had to do.

"Have a good time," said Jack Bennett with a brave smile. "We have a long drive ahead, and we can't stay around much longer anyway."

Then, after an ambiguous pause, Susan Bennett with her left hand took her husband by the crook of his arm; they exchanged one more look—that same unnerving look again!—and then they walked away.

As they proceeded down the corridor, Bennett held his breath, praying that they would escape the keen intuitive apparatus of Leskov, and this they may or may not have done; in any case, Leskov made no attempt to engage them, except by way of a sly glance out of the corner of his eye as they passed.

A CITY, A MAN

In the dim corridor Leskov touched Bennett's arm with solemnity and, after a significant pause, said, "That was the best play I ever saw."

He said it mysteriously and softly and, without allowing time for a response, added that perhaps he would come later to the party, and then he turned and walked away, with a slow satirical swagger, which appeared to Bennett to have been executed for the sole purpose of mocking his own fascinated gaze.

"Was that Leskov?" said Dicataldo, coming out of the dressing room and gazing grimly down the corridor at the well-lit entry, in which Leskov had just made a turn to the left, stepping out of sight.

Bennett checked an urge to run down the corridor in pursuit. "Yes," he said.

"What did he want."

"He didn't want anything. He just came to congratulate me on the play."

"Nice," said Dicataldo with a sneer.

"What are you driving at?"

"If you and I work on another show, I don't want him around. Leskov is a bad customer, and he messes with people's heads."

"He has never interfered with our work."

"He interfered last night."

"How?"

"Where did you and he go after the dress rehearsal."

"What's the difference? He didn't interfere with the rehearsal, did he?"

"Where did you go."

"No place. A couple of bars."

"What for."

"What is this, an inquisition?"

"You were supposed to go home and get some rest. I told everybody to go home and rest, didn't I."

"I slept all day today."

"You were supposed to be in class."

"What are you, my mother?"

"Worse. If you want me to direct your next show, you're going to have to play by the rules. Otherwise you will have to get yourself another director."

"You yourself wanted me to go to a bar last night, so what are you talking about?"

"I would have had a couple of beers with you and got you home before ten. Leskov kept you out till all hours. You could have blown the whole show tonight."

"But I didn't, did I."

"No. You were very good, but if you had slept last night instead of all day, you could have been better. You walked around the stage like a zombie until the second act."

"I did not! I was wide awake as soon as the curtain came up!"

"If you're half asleep, you don't know what you are. You may think you're wide awake, but you may not look wide awake. That's what I am here for. I tell you what you look like."

"How do you know I was up till all hours?"

"I have friends. They saw you."

"They saw me where?"

"In a bar."

"What bar?"

"Smitty's. Also The Robin's Nest."

"In both places? What were they doing, following me?"

"I have friends in many bars."

"What did all these friends of yours say I was doing?"

Dicataldo paused, apparently disquieted by the question.

"Nothing," he said after a moment. "They just saw you."

"They saw me with Leskov."

"Yes."

"And you don't like that."

"And I don't like that."

"Because you don't like Leskov."

"Because I don't like Leskov."

"Because he messes with people's heads."

"Because he messes with *your* head."

"And how do you know that?"

"Man, you . . . you are so . . . so naive!" said Dicataldo, slamming his hand against the wall. "I bet you don't have even the faintest *clue* why Leskov turned up outside the theater last night and took you around the bars and kept you up till dawn and got you so out of it that . . . that you almost blew the whole damn play!"

"Why did he."

"Because this play is yours, your property, and it's a valuable property, and it pays you dividends, and Leskov is jealous of you."

"How do you know that?"

"What are you, blind? It's written all over his face!"

"I think you're inventing."

"I'm not inventing!" shouted Dicataldo in exasperation, the blood rushing to his face.

At this point the cast came pouring out of the dressing room, some still in costume and makeup and some not, all in high spirits, and ready to go to the cast party, which was to be held about three blocks from campus at the apartment of Charlene Gallagher, a twenty-year-old matronly student, who had played the part of the aunt.

"Are you two still arguing?" said Charlene.

"If they are," said the actress who had played Anna, "I'm going to go hang myself."

There was general laughter all around.

"Quiet, quiet, everyone!" said the actor who had played the mayor. He was tall and heavy-set and had a booming voice, and he got everyone's attention. He held up a black cape for all to see.

"Ooh . . . ahh . . . " said the cast.

The actor who had played the mayor placed the cape ceremoniously around Dicataldo's shoulders. Then he held up a sleek black wig and placed that on Dicataldo's head. The wig was almost shoulder-length and covered the ears.

Dicataldo cut a villainous, operatic figure in the wig and cape, and the cast cheered.

"By the authority vested in me by the corrupt government of North Dakota," boomed the actor who had played the mayor, "I hereby order these two gentlemen, Anthony Francis Dicataldo and David Abraham Bennett, immediately to cease and desist from the intolerable argumentative discourse in which they have been engaged throughout the last two months of rehearsal!"

"Hear, hear!" cried the cast.

"I also order that compensation be made to the cast for the deep psychological injuries they have suffered as a result of said argumentative discourse!"

"Hear, hear!"

"I also order that this compensation be made in the form of a performance of the monologue of the mad professor in the absurd comedy *The Lesson,* by Eugene Ionesco, and that this performance be performed perforce by Anthony Francis Dicataldo himself at the apartment of the gracious Charlene Gallagher in no less than sixty minutes from the present moment!"

"Hear, hear!"

Dicataldo smiled and made a low bow to the company.

63

The cast applauded.

"What about Bennett?" cried the actor who had played Time and the jailer. "Doesn't Bennett have to pay?"

"Bennett has already paid!" pronounced the actor who had played the mayor.

What does he mean by that? wondered Bennett. How have I paid?

"Let's go, let's go!" shouted the two actors who had played the nephews, and they began to dance ahead down the corridor.

The rest of the cast followed.

"Wait for me!" said Bennett, and he ducked into the dressing room to get his jacket and his airline bag; then he ran back out and, catching up with the cast midway down the corridor, plunged into the center of the crowd and put one arm around the short plump redhaired actress who had played Anna.

On the way to the party, with the warm bodies of the disorderly cast pressing him on all sides, he managed to take in some of the festive spirit. Also he managed to laugh a little, to make a few jokes about the raindrops on the trees in the damp suburban streets, and to quiet, to a certain extent, the anxious inner voice nagging him over his failure to extract from either Leskov or Dicataldo any clue to the forgotten episode of the previous night.

When half an hour later Leskov turned up at the party, he turned up in the company of another graduate student, Jimmy Fisher, whose arrival took Bennett by surprise.

As Fisher followed uncertainly at Leskov's heels across the room, he appeared to Bennett to be something like a ghost, a friendly deferential ghost to be sure, but a ghost all the same, and therefore peculiar and unsettling.

Last year there had been a six or seven-week period, in March and April, when Fisher and Bennett had engaged one another with an intensity unprecedented in Bennett's experience, and perhaps Fisher's as well. In that period they found themselves swept up in a running dialogue, the compelling life of which lay not so much in the conflict of their separate views, as in the conflict they had in joint opposition to others, and in a mutual passionate desire to sort out the shades of value in everything under the sun. They talked in luncheonettes, in bars, in hallways, in the school cafeteria, and in the streets. Everywhere they met, they talked. They talked for hours on end, and they talked as urgently as ambitious generals planning the invasion of a well-defended city. About a week before the Easter vacation, however, for no apparent reason a cloud of estrangement descended on them, a gray mood, a peculiar suspiciousness, an insincerity and dullness in the tone of their speech, and then the Easter vacation came up and Fisher went out of town for two weeks. On his return he announced that he had decided to pursue a career in microbiology and was going to drop out of the humanities program and enroll in the science program instead. From then on, until the end of the semester, he cut most of his classes, and every weekend he left town, and this year he lost contact with everybody in humanities except Leskov.

Leskov and Fisher had been the only two married students in the humanities program last year, and this distinction created between them, and also between their wives, a human bond that had survived the conversion to science. Once or twice a month the Leskovs and the Fishers played bridge together, and on Columbus Day they went on a picnic, just the two couples and little Annie, in the state park about seventy-five miles up the highway.

Like Bennett, Fisher had finished his undergraduate work in three years, and he was now twenty-one. However, he looked sixteen. He was slender and lithe and had very smooth clear skin and large almond-shaped eyes and long dark lashes, and the shape of his lips was of the type classically compared with the bow of Cupid. The general opinion among his fellow students was that all in all, feature for feature, his physical appearance either was, or ought to have been, the envy of his wife, a tall thin severe woman named Olive, who worked for the county as a court stenographer and was eight years his senior.

Leskov approached Bennett with a smile and, placing one hand on Fisher's shoulder, said, "Look who's here."

As Fisher and Bennett nodded a silent uneasy greeting at each other, Leskov surveyed them with an air of paternal tenderness, and then, leaning close to Bennett, said in an undertone, "You don't belong with these people."

"Which people?" said Bennett.

Leskov ignored the question. "Let's go for a drive," he said.

"Which people?" persisted Bennett.

"Olive is under the weather," said Leskov, "and Jimmy wants me to drive him home."

"I'm having a good time," said Bennett resolutely.

Leskov signaled Fisher with a conspiratorial glance, then shrugged his shoulders, turned around and walked away. He walked with his chin up, passing imperially through the crowd and out the door.

"Dammit," muttered Bennett.

Fisher took Bennett's hand nervously. "I wanted to talk to you about your play, but . . . but Olive has a . . . a virus . . . and I'm worried about her . . . "

"Hang around for a few minutes and we'll talk," said Bennett, looking over the heads of the crowd and hoping that Leskov might reappear in the entry.

"I can't . . . honest . . . "

Bennett gave up on Leskov and directed a look of fury at Fisher. "Why? She's not dying, is she?"

"I . . . don't want to keep Leskov waiting . . . "

"Leskov can wait three minutes. I haven't talked to you in six months! Jesus, your hands are trembling. What's wrong?"

Fisher let go of Bennett's hand. "Nothing . . . I . . . forget it . . . "

"Come on, Fisher, talk to me."

"I . . . it's . . . this is just not a good time . . . "

"Were you at the play? Did you see the play?"

"Yes, of course. I just told you I did. I wouldn't have missed it for anything."

"Well? What did you think?"

"I can't tell you in just a . . . a word . . . I need to sit down and talk with you about it . . . "

"Did you like it?"

"Yes, I . . . I . . . I did . . . look, I can't talk now . . . I have a lot to say about the play . . . a lot . . . but not now . . . I can't!"

"Okay, okay. Settle down. Forget about the play. Can't you at least give me a hint about what's going on with you? You look so out of it!"

"I'm just upset . . . that's all . . . upset about . . . about Olive."

"Really? That's all?"

"Yes . . . honest . . . "

"She must have some cold. What's the matter, did she run out of Kleenex?"

Agitated, Fisher took Bennett's hand again. "Look, I can't talk anymore . . . not right now . . . but I will . . . later . . . later I'll talk . . . I promise . . . but look, it was a . . . a terrific play . . . honest . . . I . . . terrific . . . but I have to go . . . okay?"

Fisher let go of Bennett's hand, looked around at the crowd and then, backing away with trepidation, added, "You'll hear from me . . . honest . . . I promise . . . "

Cautiously he began to sidestep through the crowd, making an apology to each person he touched along the way. At the door he hesitated and for nearly a minute gazed abstractly at his own feet. Then all of a sudden his face wrinkled up into an ugly expression of impatience and he turned and left the room.

Bennett cursed under his breath, pushed his way through the crowd and hurried out into the vestibule.

"Dammit, Fisher," he shouted down the stairs, "tell Leskov to wait for me! I'll be right down!"

From a collection of about thirty jackets piled on a double bed in the bedroom, Bennett took his own, a light waterproof distinguishable from four others in the pile only by the pencil stub and scraps of paper in the righthand pocket, and walked over to a small alcove off the far side of the room; here he found Dicataldo, alone, muttering to himself and pacing up and down with a dancing limp, dressed in the black cape and wig, and also big false eyebrows.

"I'm going out for a while," said Bennett.

Dicataldo stopped pacing. "You'll miss my mad professor bit," he said.

"When are you doing it?"

"In a few minutes."

"I'll be back before the party's over."

"Where are you going, dammit."

"Just out."

"You're going with Leskov."

"I'll be back," said Bennett.

Dicataldo nodded, gazing at the floor. Then he looked up at Bennett, then down at the floor again, and in a gratuitous gesture of disgust tore off the wig and the false eyebrows and walked out of the alcove in the guise of his everyday persona—whose limp was subtler and grimmer, whose hair was blacker, and whose large dark deepset eyes were more haunted and implacable without the false eyebrows than with.

Bennett stared after him anxiously and, after deliberating a moment, went and got his airline bag from the floor at the foot of the bed and set off once again through the crowd in the livingroom, managing along the way to apologize to a few members of the cast, most of whom were involved in an improvised burlesque that entailed calling each other by the names of their characters and throwing shoes and empty beercans at each other, and then he left.

He found Leskov sitting alone on the front steps, smoking a cigarette.

"Where's Fisher?"

Without replying, Leskov stood up and walked to his Buick, which was parked across the street. He got in behind the wheel and started the engine.

After a moment Bennett followed, getting in the front seat on the passenger side, and repeated the question about Fisher.

"He was in a hurry," said Leskov.

"But he lives almost five miles from here."

"He had his car around the corner."

Bennett was bewildered. "I thought you said you were driving him home."

Leskov drove slowly around the perimeter of the campus, steering with the bottom of one wrist on top of the wheel and now and then weaving idly back and forth across the center of the road.

"You should know something about Fisher," he said.

"Go ahead."

"If it gets back to him that I let it out, it will hurt him bad."

70

"I won't say a word."

"Swear."

"I swear."

"Fisher has a thing for a guy he played tennis with at the University of New Hampshire."

"What kind of thing?"

"They write letters to each other in care of the post office."

Bennett kept silent for a moment; then he said, "Where's the guy?"

"He's in New Hampshire with a wife and a kid. Last week he tried to kill himself."

"Does Olive know?"

"Her cunt knows." After a pause Leskov added, "You don't seem surprised."

Before Bennett had a chance to decide whether or not he was surprised, and just as the Buick was passing the stone arch that was the main entrance to the campus, Leskov abruptly took his foot off the accelerator, put his right hand on his ribs and gasped in pain, squinting his eyes and baring his teeth in a sort of grin.

"What's wrong!" said Bennett in alarm.

Leskov turned the wheel with his left hand, keeping his right hand on his ribs, made a U-turn and went through the stone arch into the circular drive by the administration building and parked at an odd angle a few yards from the curb. He switched off the motor, leaving the headlights on, and opened the door, then sat very still with his eyes shut and breathed methodically.

"Are you all right?" said Bennett, leaning over to shut off the headlights.

Leskov opened his eyes. "I have to pee," he said.

He got out of the car and started to walk toward the building. Lights were on here and there along the first floor, though the rest of the building was dark. He went up four stone steps to the main entrance. The big high doors were wide open, and Bennett could see a custodian mopping the floor in the lobby. As Leskov entered, the custodian assumed a military posture, holding the mop like a lancer at parade rest.

Bennett got out of the car and hurried up the steps.

"It's all right, Eddy," he called out reassuringly. "This man is a student here and a friend of mine."

"Okay if you say so," said the custodian.

"We just want to use the men's room."

"I lock up in fifteen minutes."

Bennett and Leskov went into the building.

"How come he knows you and not me?" said Leskov.

"I'm a friendly person," said Bennett.

"Which way?"

"It's in the east wing."

"I didn't bring my compass."

"To your left." Bennett led the way and pointed out the door to the men's room.

Leskov went in and came out a moment later.

"I can't find the light," he said.

Bennett went in and turned on the light.

"Magic," he said.

Leskov went to one of the urinals and relieved himself.

At the washbasin he squeezed some green liquid soap from a glass dispenser on the wall and looked in the mirror at Bennett's face.

"I'm doing this all wrong," he said.

"I don't know what you're talking about."

"I'm talking about, like, I ought to wash my hands first, before, not after I touch my cock."

Before getting back on the road, Leskov tuned the car radio to a popular music program and set the volume high enough to preclude conversation, but as soon as he pulled up to the curb in front of his apartment, which was one half of a one-story duplex made of white stucco, about half a mile from the campus, he turned the radio off, leaving the motor and headlights on, and sat quietly for a few moments, gazing at the house. There was light in the windows, and the Venetian blinds were shut.

"You look tired," said Bennett. "Maybe you ought to call it a night."

"Sarah loved the play," said Leskov, "and she wants to tell you."

"Are you sure she's still up?"

"Listen to me . . . " Leskov turned to glare at Bennett with unaccountable ferocity.

"I'm listening."

"She's up."

Leskov shut off the motor and the lights and got out of the car.

Bennett followed, feeling nervous and wishing that he had remained at the party.

On the doorstep he said, "Before we go in, I . . . I want to ask you something about . . . about . . . "

"What!"

"About last night. I was sort of out of it, and I think there may have been some things I said and did that you could take the wrong way."

After a pause Leskov said, "Could I?"

"Well, I . . . look, there is something I . . . I can't remember . . . it's really not important, except that . . . it's been nagging me all day. The last place we were at last night? Remember? I think I lost some lecture notes in that place. They were on index cards. I had them in my jacket pocket, and they must have fallen out. I want to go back tomorrow and see if the cards are there, but I don't remember what street the place was on. Do you remember the name of the street?"

Leskov appeared to be angered by the question. After some deliberation he glared at Bennett and replied with contempt, "I'll write down the address for you."

At first Bennett took the reply to be a typical example of Leskov's annoying trick of deflecting an ordinary question with a cryptic sarcasm, but then, a moment later, as Leskov was putting his key in the door, Bennett began to have second thoughts, speculating that perhaps the reply had been intended not sarcastically, but sincerely, and that Leskov in actual fact preferred to write rather than say the address. But why would he prefer to write rather than say the address? Why couldn't he have just this once answered a normal question in a normal way like a normal person!

Leskov turned the key and pushed the door, which opened directly onto the livingroom.

With a swift change in mood he cried out, "Look who's here!" and, smiling broadly, pressed Bennett in the small of the back and urged him inside.

At a desk made of two sawhorses and a door sat Leskov's wife Sarah, who swung her legs around at once and stood up with suspended breath, gripping the carriage of her small Olivetti typewriter in one hand, while Robert Orbach, a pale thin redhaired man seated on a sofa against the far wall, merely crossed one leg over the other, rearranging the yellow notepad in his lap, and looked up impassively.

"Hi," he said.

"Hi," said Bennett. He turned to Sarah. "Hi," he added.

"Hi," she said.

"Hi, hi," said Leskov satirically.

Sarah looked at Bennett. "Come sit down," she said.

Bennett glanced briefly at Leskov, then crossed the room, pausing before the sofa to examine the rebellious and florid scrawl on the notepad in Orbach's lap.

"Is that the chapter on Kant?" he said.

"If you read it upside-down like that," said Leskov, "it's a Chinese puzzle. If you read it right-side up, it's a pile of ashes."

Bennett winced, and a lump appeared in his throat.

"I think it's wonderful," said Sarah.

"Gimme a kiss," Leskov said.

Sarah went to him with a bright smile and took his face in her hands, apishly puckering her lips to give him a brief kiss on the side of the nose.

Leskov smiled and blushed. "What about some cheese and crackers," he said.

"I'll slice up a cucumber too," she said.

She turned her back to Leskov, smiled furtively at Bennett and walked across the room.

She walked purposefully and with apparent pleasure, with her toes turned out, like a ballerina on holiday. Just before the doorway to the kitchen she paused for a moment to straighten a little picture in a wood frame on the wall. This picture, which she had made herself, was the only evidence in the house that once she had studied art and had six years ago taken a bachelor's degree in art education from Boston University. The subject of the picture was three fishing boats in a sunny harbor, and the medium was pale watercolors with a few deft penstrokes in black ink.

When Sarah had disappeared into the kitchen, Bennett said, "Have you got a cigarette?"

Leskov ignored the request and turned to Orbach. "How's it going?"

"In the commentary you're okay so far," said Orbach, "but in the citations I found one mistranslation."

"Did you change it?"

"Of course."

Leskov reached into his shirt pocket for a pack of cigarettes, gave one cigarette to Bennett without looking at him and went and leaned on the arm of the sofa to examine the change, which Orbach explained in a light playful style, tapping the notepad with the eraser end of a blue pencil.

Bennett was confused and distressed by the general atmosphere in the room. Nothing out of the ordinary had happened in the few minutes since his arrival, and yet everything had a fantastic dream-like quality, perhaps in part because nobody had mentioned the play. Why had nobody mentioned the play?

He moved quietly to the homemade desk, put his airline bag on the floor, and picked up a matchbook that lay near a small stack of typewritten pages piled face down beside the Olivetti. He tore out one match, struck it and, pretending to be interested only in lighting the cigarette, turned his back to shield his hands from Leskov's view. He shook the match once to extinguish it and dropped it in an ashtray; then, deftly, silently, he flipped the stack of pages face up to reveal the title page, which read: *Chapter Four: THE HOLY KANT.*

At that moment he was alerted by the sound of a door opening; quickly he turned around and discovered, not without some surprise and anxiety, a barefoot young woman, dressed in a wrinkled white shirt and bluejeans, walking idly through the doorway from the bedroom, rubbing her eyes and yawning, and Orbach sitting as if pinned to the sofaback and gazing at her in terror.

"Hi," she said.

As she opened her mouth apparently to add something to her greeting, she was interrupted by a hiccough, which she attempted to suppress by holding her breath and putting the fingertips of one hand on her mouth; but then still another hiccough escaped her, and she took her hand from her mouth and laughed girlishly.

Sarah returned from the kitchen with a tray of crackers and cheese and slices of cucumber.

77

"Hi, Alice," she said.

"I'm going for a walk," said Orbach, and he stood up. "I'll be back in half an hour."

Sarah put the tray on the coffee table. "Nobody goes anywhere till they eat," she said.

"Let him alone," said Leskov.

Alice went to Orbach, maternally stroked the back of his neck and, after whispering something in his ear, led him to the kitchen.

Alice and Orbach had both done their undergraduate work in Florida, but in different towns, and had never met before entering graduate school in New York. In New York, Florida provided them with ground for friendship, and they had been like brother and sister and an odd item for nearly a year and a half. Orbach was cool, pallid, and dry, with skin like cellophane, a prodigy in math and musicology, and also a polyglot, and he had not yet picked a thesis topic. Alice was warm, ruddy, and humid, and, having read herself into a submissive passion for the poetry of Baudelaire and the plays of Eugene O'Neill, had recently declared that she would do her thesis on one or the other. For various reasons she and Orbach had been spending a lot of time this semester in the Leskov home and had come to assume easy family relations with the refrigerator, the telephone, and the bath.

"What was that about?" said Bennett, as soon as Alice and Orbach were out of the room.

"He's in love with her and he's upset," said Sarah.

"Why is he upset?"

"He found out she's got a wart on her ass," Leskov said.

"She's pregnant," said Sarah.

"She can't be," said Bennett. "Since when?"

Sarah bit into a slice of cucumber. "It's almost three months," she said.

"When did she find out?"

"Three weeks ago," said Sarah.

Bennett looked at her in surprise. "Are you sure she's known for three weeks?"

"Yes."

"Is Orbach the father?" said Bennett.

"She never slept with him. She's not sure who the father is. She says there are five or six possibilities."

"Have a cracker," Leskov said sharply.

"But she came to me just last week and asked me to sleep with her," said Bennett. "She told me she was a virgin and . . . and wanted me to be her first man!"

"Yeah, but you turned her down, you prick," said Leskov.

Bennett turned to Leskov. "Also she said that you told her I was in love with her."

Leskov lifted an eyebrow in mock surprise. "Yeah?" he said.

"Yeah."

"So?"

"So I never told you that."

"Sorry," said Leskov, "My mistake."

"Did you know she was pregnant then?" said Bennett.

"She's in love with you."

"I know she's in love with me, but I'm not in love with her."

"If you don't marry her, she's going to have a bastard in six months."

"But I'm not the father!"

"What's the difference?"

"Wait a second. You mean you were trying to trick me into sleeping with her so that I'd think I was the father and then marry her?"

"Dimitri," said Sarah, "you didn't do that, did you?"

"The kid's a neurotic," said Leskov.

"What's going on here?" said Bennett.

"Shh," said Sarah. "They'll hear."

"Why didn't you set her up with Orbach?" said Bennett. "Orbach's in love with her."

"Orbach's no good for her," said Leskov.

"What's wrong with him?" said Bennett.

"He's from Sweetwater."

"So what? She's from Key West."

"They got sailors in Key West."

"What the hell are you talking about?"

"I'm talking in shorthand."

"I don't understand shorthand. Say it in plain English."

"In plain English they're a bad match," said Leskov.

"That's a lot of crap."

"Watch your mouth in front of my wife."

"Sorry, Sarah," said Bennett.

"You have to be kidding," said Sarah.

"Besides," said Leskov, "Orbach is already married to the goddam encyclopedia."

Orbach and Alice returned to the room, holding hands, and there followed an uneasy silence, which

Orbach broke rather awkwardly by asking Bennett whether he'd been satisfied with the performance of his play tonight.

Bennett was taken off guard by the question. "Weren't you there?" he said.

Orbach lowered his eyes. "No," he said. "Sorry."

"Dimitri has to have his paper in tomorrow," explained Sarah. "We're going to be up all night finishing it."

"You mean . . . you didn't go either?" said Bennett.

"I wanted to," said Sarah. "I'd been looking forward to it for weeks. Really. It's just that this paper is due, and we left it to the last minute, like always."

Bennett turned to Leskov in disbelief. "Out in the car you said that Sarah loved the play and wanted to tell me. Didn't you say that?"

"Sure she loves the play," said Leskov. "You gave her the script two months ago, didn't you."

"But she already told me she liked the script," said Bennett, and he felt the lump return to his throat, and he was afraid suddenly that he might at any moment begin to cry like a child.

"She wanted to tell you again," said Leskov.

"But she could have gone to see the play! She wanted to see it! Didn't you?"

"Yes," said Sarah. "But Dimitri's paper is due in the thesis class tomorrow."

"That paper is not due for another six days," said Bennett. "I haven't got mine done either. Nobody in the whole damn class does! Ask Orbach. Orbach, are the papers due tomorrow?"

"They're due next Monday," said Orbach, nervously avoiding Leskov's eyes.

"That's six days from now," said Bennett.

"You mean I could have gone to the play?" said Sarah, shyly, to Leskov.

"I need to look the paper over after it's typed," said Leskov, "and I need some time to think about it before it's turned in."

"Were you there, Alice?" said Bennett.

"I wanted to come," said Alice. "But Dimitri asked me to babysit. Then when I got here, there was a change in plans and I stuck around to tell Annie a bedtime story and put her to sleep while Sarah and Bobby worked on the paper, and then I fell asleep myself."

"So nobody went," said Bennett. "Terrific."

"I went," said Leskov.

"Look, why did you drag me out of the party? I was having a good time. Tonight was opening and closing night, and I wanted to celebrate. I wanted to hear what people thought of my play!"

"It's a great play," said Leskov in a sad and tender voice.

The doorbell began to ring violently. Sarah gasped, putting one hand on her chest, then hurried to the door and pulled it open.

On the threshhold stood Olive Fisher, clad in a maroon sweater, nicely tailored maroon slacks, gray shoes, and a gray bandana wrapped around her hair with a few brown curls sprung loose over her forehead and ears. In public Olive customarily wore a necklace and makeup, but now her neck was bare and appeared to be preternaturally long and thin, and her lips were pale, her nose red, her eyes naked and tearful.

She stepped inside and pushed the door shut with one hand behind her back.

"I want you to read this," she said, thrusting a folded piece of white paper into Sarah's hand.

Sarah, intimidated, unfolded the paper, squinted at it and, while walking absently about the room, read aloud in a hoarse voice, inflecting each statement as a question.

Dear Olive,

You are very dear to me but I don't want to be married anymore so I'm going away. The money in the savings account is yours and if you need more, let me know by writing me a letter in care of the Leskovs. Dimitri has my address, but I've made him promise to keep it secret, so please don't pressure him. I believe I've made a decision that in the long run will benefit both of us.

With devotion and love,

Jimmy

Sarah blinked. "I didn't know anything about this," she said.

"Twenty minutes ago my doorbell rang," said Olive. "I went to answer it and found that letter on the step and saw Jimmy driving away in the Plymouth."

She put her eyes in her fists and began to sob.

Sarah took her arm. "Here, come sit down."

Olive shook her head in protest, dabbed at her nose and eyes with a useless wad of Kleenex and, for the first time, looked at Leskov.

"You were with him tonight, I believe," she said.

"Mm." Leskov examined her a moment, then turned his back, rolling his eyes in a slapstick style, and casually walked to the far corner of the room, where he let himself down with an air of weary resignation into a modern easy chair that was made of one black iron ring tilted like the orbit of a planet on a map, four black iron legs, and a few yards of beige canvass that served as the seat and the backrest.

Olive glared at him. "What happened between the two of you tonight?" she said.

"Sarah," said Leskov, "bring Olive a glass of brandy."

"I don't want a glass of brandy," said Olive.

"Bring her some hot tea then."

"I'm asking you a question."

"Olive, Olive," said Leskov with a melancholy paternal nod of the head.

"I'll get some tea," said Sarah.

"I don't want any tea!" said Olive. "How can you let him order you around like this?"

"He's not ordering me," said Sarah.

"I'll get the tea for you myself," said Leskov, and he stood up and, lifting his shoulders, extended his right hand to show the palm as a sign of conciliation.

"You're behind all this," said Olive.

"I'll get the tea."

"I don't want any tea! I just want you to admit what you did to my marriage!"

"What did I do to it?"

"The same thing you did to Robert Frost!"

"Ah . . ."

"First you did it to Robert Frost, you bastard, and then you did it to my marriage. Admit it!"

"Let me tell you something, Olive," said Leskov. "I've done many things in my life, but not one of them did I do to Robert Frost. Believe me, I don't even know the guy. Ask Sarah. Sarah, do I know Robert Frost?"

Olive narrowed her eyes shrewdly. "You know what I mean," she said.

"This is a statement I can refute with some authority," said Leskov.

"Jimmy used to love Robert Frost," said Olive. "He used to worship him. He has half the poems memorized."

"I know."

"But what you don't know is that one day a couple of weeks ago he came home from school and said, 'Robert Frost writes like a farmer.' He just walked in the kitchen and said it out of the blue. 'Robert Frost writes like a farmer.' He didn't even say hello."

"That's bad manners," said Leskov.

"That's not the point."

"What's the point?"

"The point is that it wasn't Jimmy talking. It was you, Dimitri. It was your voice."

"I've never been in your kitchen, Olive."

"It gave me a chill in my spine."

Leskov laughed aloud.

"Dimitri," cautioned Sarah.

"What are you laughing about?" said Olive.

"You've got it all wrong, Olive," said Leskov. "Me, I like Robert Frost. Two yellow roads in the forest and all that."

" 'Two roads diverged in a yellow wood,' " corrected Olive.

"Yeah. Beautiful stuff."

"Jimmy's grandfather was a farmer."

"I know. And so was George Washington."

"Jimmy loved his grandfather," said Olive indignantly, and she clenched her fists.

"Listen, Olive . . . wait right here. I'll be right back. Sarah, don't let her leave." With this Leskov hurried out to the bedroom and returned a moment later carrying three suits on hangers. "Look at this stuff, Olive," he said, showing one of the suits like a salesman. "Each one of these costumes cost me four-and-a-half bills and I got nine more in the closet. I got one in there that cost me seven! And you know what? It pinches in the crotch."

Olive turned to Sarah and said, "He talks like a gangster." Then, turning back to Leskov, Olive said, "You're supposed to be studying for a doctorate in philosophy, and you talk like a gangster."

"Yeah."

"Frankly I think it's an affectation."

"She's right!" said Leskov with a grand sweep of the hands. "You're absolutely right, Olive! Really, you hit the head on the nail!"

"The nail on the head," corrected Olive.

"That too," said Leskov.

Leskov studied the floor a moment and then glanced at Olive out of the corner of his eye. "So listen, Olive dear," he said. "Do you want me to tell you where Jimmy is?"

"You mean you would?" said Olive in amazement.

"Sure!" cried Leskov. "Are you kidding? Why not?"

86

"Well . . . I thought . . . "

"Listen, Olive, do you know Heidegger?"

"Heidegger?"

"Yes."

"Why?"

"It's important."

"Heidegger, Heidegger . . . yes, of course. It's a city . . . in Austria."

"Yeah?"

"Oh, my God," said Olive, placing one hand on her breast. "Is that where Jimmy has gone? To Austria?"

"Well, no."

"Then why are you asking me about Heidegger?"

Suddenly Leskov appeared to be plunged into a deep melancholy. "Olive, I've got to tell you something," he said.

"What?"

"Heidegger is not in Austria."

Olive blushed. "It's not?"

Leskov blushed in return and looked at her sympathetically. "Well, I mean, like, the famous one, yeah, that's in Austria. I mean, like, you're absolutely right about that, Olive. The famous Heidegger, that's in Austria. But see, I'm talking about a different Heidegger. A different Heidegger altogether."

Olive regained her composure and attempted to disguise a sigh of relief. "I didn't know there were two Heideggers," she said.

"Oh, yeah, there are Heideggers all over the place."

"Where is the one you mean?"

"Germany."

"I have never heard of it," said Olive with haughty grandeur. "Is it a very small city?"

"No, it's a man."

"A man?"

"Yes."

Olive examined Leskov suspiciously. "What sort of a man?"

"A philosopher. Big phenomenologist with a private practice. Very seminal."

"What does he have to do with Jimmy?"

"Well . . ."

"Has Jimmy gone off to Germany to study with this person? Is that it? Is that what you're trying to tell me?"

"No, no, wait. You're getting ahead of me, Olive."

"Can't you just tell me straight out where Jimmy is?"

"I'm trying to, Olive, but it's complicated. I need to fill you in with a few details first, okay?"

Olive tightened her jaw and strained against impatience. "Just get on with it."

"All right. Now answer me this: Do you know Saratoga?"

"If you mean the city in the center of this state, yes. My maternal grandmother lives there. Also it is said to be the place in which Ulysses S. Grant died."

"Right!" cried Leskov with exaggerated delight. "That's exactly the Saratoga I mean! All right! Now we're getting somewhere! Now, answer me this: Do you know Heshel Brustein?"

"No."

"Nothing?"

"Well, I know *of* him. Jimmy mentioned the name."

"I thought so. What did Jimmy tell you about Heshel?"

"Nothing. Just that he lives in Saratoga."

"You call that nothing?"

"Frankly, yes."

"But don't you see how the pieces are starting to fit together?" said Leskov, and he began to tick off each of the "pieces" on his fingers. "First you got Saratoga. Then you got Heshel Brustein. Then you got Heshel Brustein *lives* in Saratoga! See? See how it's fitting together?"

"Has Jimmy gone to Saratoga? Is that what you're hinting at?"

"Wait. What else did Jimmy tell you about Heshel?"

"That he's a German. A Jew. A German Jew. Also a philosopher."

"Right. A German, A Jew. A German Jew," said Leskov with a merry sing-song lilt in his voice, as if reciting a nursery rhyme. Then he sobered abruptly and, squinting significantly at Olive, added, "Compared to Heidegger, though, as a philosopher Heshel is not so big. I mean, he is not *sem*inal, see?"

"Why did you bring the suits out?"

"I'm getting to that. Here, Sarah dear, take the suits. My arms are killing me."

Sarah took the suits and laid them on the sofa.

"I hope this is leading somewhere," said Olive. "Does Heshel Brustein know where Jimmy is? And what does this Heidegger person have to do with it! You're confusing me!"

"Heshel studied with Heidegger back in the early thirties," said Leskov. "He knew Heidegger personally, you see, and a lot of the early stuff that Heshel wrote was under the influence of the master. The later stuff, though, is pure Heshel. Mainly he does demolition jobs. Like, first he does a number on Descartes, then he does a number on Hegel, then he does a number on Kant. Like that. One after the other he busts their balls. Anyway, Olive, now Heshel Brustein lives in Saratoga. Just like you said. And this is very important. And when I found out, I said to Jimmy, 'What the hell is Heshel Brustein doing in Saratoga? That's where the goddam racetrack is!' 'Who is Heshel Brustein?' said Jimmy. 'He writes books,' I said, 'and we gotta go see him.' So I wrote a letter, and Heshel wrote back, and me and Jimmy we got in the Plymouth, and before we knew it, we were in Saratoga. And there was Heshel Brustein. Teaching at Skidmore. Phenomenology. With one lung. And a broken back. And a twisted leg. I mean, he was beautiful. Do you know about this trip, Olive?"

"I know that Jimmy went, and that he got home at one in the morning, that's all. He didn't ever really tell me what happened."

"Well, I am going to tell you, Olive. I am going to tell you what happened. Jimmy, see, he was very quiet. But me, I have a mouth, and I talked and talked. And Heshel, he also talked. Except that Heshel didn't just talk. He, like, *spoke*. Very formidable. Anyway, me and Heshel we went on about this thing and that thing, and finally after a while I said to him, 'Look, Doctor Brustein, I read all your books, and I think you're terrific, and what I'd like to know is: What is your opinion of Heidegger?' And . . . and

. . . listen to this, Olive . . . this is the whole point: Heshel, he looked at me, then he looked at Jimmy, then he looked again at me, then he bent forward in his chair and put one hand on my knee, and he said, 'Mister Leskov, let me tell you something: I shit on Heidegger.' Like that! I shit on Heidegger! Then suddenly he squinted at Jimmy and said, 'What is wrong, Mister Fisher? Are you ill?' So I turned my head, and what did I see? I saw Jimmy with all the blood drained out of his face and his eyes like pies, and I said to myself, 'Uh-oh, he's gonna pass out.' But he didn't. That's it. That's the story."

"I don't understand," said Olive.

"That may be," said Leskov.

"What do the suits have to do with it?"

"I like expensive clothes. I am in debt for forty thousand dollars. These are facts."

"You're insane."

"This is a view you may hold, and you may even hold it in good faith, but only if you accept without doubt certain premises whose foundation is a bottomless pit."

"I thought you said you were going to tell me where Jimmy is."

"I just did," said Leskov.

"Sarah," said Olive, "what is going on here?"

"I think what Dimitri is trying to say," interrupted Bennett, after glancing at Sarah, who was frozen with anxiety, "is that this incident in Saratoga brought about some kind of a change in Jimmy . . . that it shocked him into some kind of realization. I think Dimitri is trying to say where Jimmy is . . . not geographically . . . but maybe, like, emotionally . . . or spiritually . . . something like that . . . "

"If I needed you to tell the world what I am trying to say," said Leskov with a nasty look in his eye, "I would start a petition and get you elected to the House of goddam Representatives."

"Look, man, she doesn't understand what the hell you're talking about," said Bennett, "and she's in pain."

"I know she's in pain."

"Then why are you torturing her?"

"Olive," said Leskov, "am I torturing you?"

"I don't know what you're doing," said Olive, weeping now quite defenselessly. "I don't know what you're doing, and I don't know what you're saying. What are you saying? You were the last one to see Jimmy before he left, and you had an enormous influence over him. He talked about you all the time!"

"Listen, Olive," said Leskov with an air of profound compassion. "Listen, dear. Come now, look up at me."

Olive looked up with innocent expectation, like a child.

"That's better," continued Leskov. "Now, listen. Here's the problem. All of us—you, me, everybody— all of us now and then confuse the names of things with the things themselves, and this gets us into all kinds of trouble. Like, take the name Olive. Well, if you were to ask us who you ought to marry, and we were to confuse you with your name, then we would probably advise you to marry either Popeye or a martini, right?"

Here Olive laughed through her tears, responding to both the joke and the affectionate tone in which Leskov was now speaking.

"Right," she said, and she dried her eyes and looked at him for the first time with a kind of trust and genuine good feeling. "So what are you saying?"

"What I am saying," said Leskov gently, "is that Heidegger is not a city, but a man. And your husband, Olive, is not a husband, but a cocksucker."

Leskov continued to stare at her steadily and playfully, until her face paled, and a look of unspeakable horror came into her eyes, and then he turned with the ostentatious grace of a fashion model and walked out the front door.

The others in the room, stunned, watched intently for a sign from Olive, who after a moment ran out of the house.

Bennett followed at once and called her name, but she kept running, taking quick violent breaths, as if each were to be her last. She ran across the small lawn past Leskov without looking at him and, in what appeared to be a single swift uninterrupted gesture, got into her car, a blue Chevrolet sedan, started the motor and drove away furiously, ignoring the stop sign at the corner.

"Goddammit!" said Bennett, turning to glare fiercely at Leskov.

Leskov, however, was looking elsewhere. He was looking at Orbach, Alice, and Sarah, who were gathered on the doorstep.

"Alice, I think you should go after Olive and keep her company for a while." Leskov reached into a pocket in his trousers and brought out a set of keys. "Here, you can take the Buick."

"I'll get my shoes and jacket," said Alice with gravity and disappeared into the house.

A moment later she reappeared with her shoes on, hurried down the steps, and, after pushing one arm into a jacket sleeve, took the keys from Leskov.

"Phone if you have any trouble," said Leskov.

Alice glowered at him reproachfully and got into the Buick and drove away.

"What the hell did you have to go and do that for?" said Bennett.

"I'm concerned about Olive," said Leskov. "I want Alice to comfort her."

"I'm not talking about giving the Buick to Alice, for chrissake!"

"Then what are you talking about?"

"I'm talking about what you said to Olive!"

"Listen . . ."

"It was so damn sadistic. I mean, it was like . . . it was just so damn . . . so damn sadistic! I don't understand what goes on in your head!"

"Listen to me . . ."

"What are you trying to prove? That you're smarter than Olive? That can't be it, can it? So then what is it? Are you trying to teach her something? Is that it? Did you have a purpose? A reason? Or was it just senseless cruelty! Just tell me, and whatever you say, I'll accept it."

"Yeah," said Leskov, "you'll accept it."

"I will!" insisted Bennett at the verge of tears. "Really!"

94

"I know," said Leskov with a sneer.

"Oh, for godsakes, man, what's the sneer about? I want to be friends with you, dammit, and all you can do is . . . is . . . sneer! I mean, what's the point of that! It's just . . . just more cruelty, that's all. More dumb senseless cruelty. And, like an idiot, I keep taking it! I keep taking it and taking it and taking it!"

"Dimitri, David," called Sarah from the doorstep, "come inside. The neighbors can hear every word."

Bennett looked at Sarah. "Why do I keep taking it, Sarah?" he said. "And why do you? Why do any of us!"

"I don't want to talk about it out here," said Sarah. "Now, come inside, both of you!"

Leskov smiled at her and nodded. Then he did an extraordinary thing. He placed his left foot before his right, bowed from the waist and, just before his nose touched his knee, picked a bare dandelion from the lawn. "I got a weed," he said to his shoe and closed his fist around the stem; then, rocking himself like a bowler, he swung his arm backward and forward and up and punched Bennett on the jaw, knocking him to the ground.

"Dimitri!" cried Sarah, and she rushed down the steps and hurried across the lawn.

Leskov, however, blocked her way. "It's all right," he said gently, taking her by the wrist.

"What do you mean it's all right!" she said.

"I mean let it alone," said Leskov. "He knows."

The cryptic statement, "He knows," appeared for the moment to settle the matter. Sarah, after a brief maternal glance at Bennett, turned her back, took Leskov by the hand and led him away . . . across the lawn and up to the doorstep—and the two of them disappeared into the house, followed, rather meekly, by Orbach.

Amazed, Bennett sat where he fell. He sat and contemplated the house. Twice the shadow of Sarah passed across the Venetian blinds, but they remained shut, and no other sign came from within.

After a while he put his hand in his mouth and here and there pinched his teeth. Finding them secure, he stood up, slapped the grass and dirt from the seat of his trousers and walked across the lawn, somewhat uneasily, toward the house.

As the doorbell was harsh and shrill and loud and might wake Annie, he did not ring it, but instead gave two quick raps on the door, which was opened by Sarah almost at once, as if she had anticipated his return.

She looked at him tenderly, with knitted brows.

"I just came to get my bag," he said. "My airline bag. I left it inside. I have some stuff in it that I need."

"Are you all right, David?"

"Yes . . . yes . . . fine . . . "

"Come inside."

"No. Thanks. It's a little late."

"Oh, David, you look so . . . so . . . "

"I'm fine, really. No problem."

"Please, David . . . come in . . . "

96

"No, Sarah, honest, it's not a good idea . . . not right now. Do you think you could bring my bag out to me? I'd really appreciate it. I left it under the desk."

"David, I . . . oh, damn!"

Sarah's eyes filled with tears, and she turned around and hurried away. Though she left the door half open, Bennett could no longer see her.

He heard muffled voices, talking in an agitated undertone, but he could not make out the words. After a minute or so Leskov appeared in the doorway, wearing an overcoat and a hat and holding the airline bag. Then Sarah reappeared and stood at his back, looking over his shoulder.

With a sad sober look in his eye, he peered at Bennett and said, "Wanna go for a walk?"

Bennett cast his eyes down boyishly in embarrassment and shrugged his shoulders, indicating that a walk was a thing he would not reject.

"Promise my wife you won't hit me," said Leskov. "My wife, she worries about me. 'That David,' she said, 'he has shoulders and hands like a lumberjack, and he is twice your size, and he could break you in half. He could even break that pretty nose of yours that I love so much.' Hey . . . are you listening?"

Bennett looked up at Leskov in bewilderment, then glanced at Sarah and found her smiling and rolling her eyes.

"Promise her you won't hit me," added Leskov. "Otherwise she won't let me go for a walk."

"I promise," said Bennett.

"See? He promises. Now promise me. Are you gonna hit me?"

"No."

"Promise."

"I promise."

Leskov stepped out onto the doorstep and handed Bennett the airline bag.

Sarah said, "Don't stay out too long, you two. Dimitri?"

"Yeah?"

"It's cold and damp . . . "

"Yeah?"

"Don't you want your scarf?"

"Me and the lumberjack, we don't wear scarves, right?"

"Right," said Bennett.

The two young men walked in silence for nearly two blocks. As they were turning a corner into a street that was lined, unlike any of the other streets in the neighborhood, with dark evergreen pines, Leskov paused to light a cigarette, cupping the match in two hands against the mist and a soft breeze.

"Talk to me," he said softly, as if to himself, waving the match and throwing it away.

After a moment's reflection Bennett said, "Have you got another cigarette?"

Leskov gave Bennett a cigarette and let him have a light from the cigarette that was already lit.

They started walking again.

Bennett said, "How come you tried to trick me into marrying Alice?"

"Alice is a good woman, and she loves you, and she would be good for you."

"So you admit it . . . that . . . that you tried to trick me."

"Yeah," said Leskov with a cunning sidelong glance, "but you were too smart."

"How come you did that!"

"I just told you. She would be good for you."

"Maybe she would . . . maybe she would! . . . but, if you don't mind, in the future I'd rather make my own mistakes!"

"I don't understand."

"Why? What don't you understand?"

"Well, see, I guess what you mean when you say you would rather make your own mistakes is that you would rather make a bad marriage into which you were not tricked, than a good marriage into which you were tricked. Have I got that right?"

"Yes."

"I thought so. But, see, this gives me a problem that is like a headache. So, you have to help me and answer a question: If you were tricked into a good marriage, would this good marriage be a mistake?"

"Yes."

"But, then, who would have made this mistake?"

"Me. Of course."

"Then what's the difference? If you had fallen for the trick and married Alice, you still would have made your own mistake. Isn't that right?"

"You're twisting the whole thing around!" said Bennett, after deliberating a moment in anger and confusion."

"I am?"

"Yes! And you're missing the point altogether!"

"What point?"

"The point that you are mucking around in my life, dammit, and that I don't like it!"

"Ah . . . well!" said Leskov exuberantly. "This I can understand!"

"You can?"

"Of course!"

"Then why . . . why did you do this thing?"

"I couldn't help it," said Leskov. "It's a sickness. It runs in the family."

"What? What do you mean?"

"I mean, my grandfather was a matchmaker."

"I thought you said he was a shoemaker."

"That was the grandfather on my father's side. But the grandfather on my mother's side, he was a matchmaker. Also he was a tailor. He liked to cut things up and sew them together."

In reply Bennett said nothing. He did not know what to say. He was bewildered and furious. He walked on in silence for a minute or two before he could bring himself to speak again.

"Where's Fisher?" he demanded sharply.

"He left," said Leskov, after a pause.

"Where did he go?"

"I promised I wouldn't tell."

"Did he go to New Hampshire?"

"He'll get in touch with you."

"How do you know?"

"He told me."

"When did he tell you that?"

"Tonight. After the play. The play had a big effect on him, and he wants to tell you. He says it was your play that made him decide to take off."

"He is out of his mind," said Bennett.

"Why?"

"Because my play has nothing to do with him."

"Maybe it has."

"Look, that play takes place over a hundred years ago in North Dakota! It has absolutely nothing to do with Fisher and his kind of problems!"

"It takes place in North Dakota?" Leskov made a show of amazement. "Hey, I missed that. North Dakota?"

"How could you miss it? North Dakota is mentioned at least a dozen times!"

"Yeah? North Dakota? Gee, and all along I thought it was just about these two guys from anywhere."

"There are thirty-five characters in that play."

"Yeah? Well, see, I didn't count. Thirty-five?"

"Yes."

"And they're all from North Dakota?"

"Yes."

"How about that. I bet I got the plot wrong too."

"What did you get from the plot."

"I got, like, there are these two guys. And one guy sits, and the other guy moves."

"By the guy who sits, you mean the elder brother."

"Yeah."

"And that's what the whole play comes to for you? One guy sits, and the other guy moves?"

"No. That's the first half."

"What's the second half."

101

"The second half is when the guy who sits gets up. That's the great stroke. He gets up, see, but it's too late. He's been sitting too long. And the first move he makes, it's a clumsy one, a catastrophe. And so the other guy, the guy who moves, he wins."

"He wins?"

"Yeah."

"What are you, crazy? What does he win? He gets hanged in the third act!"

"Yeah. But the guy who sits? He gets hanged in the *se*cond act. See?"

"Jesus."

"What's wrong? You look unhappy."

"I am!"

"Why?"

"Because it's a play, dammit, not a goddam contest!"

"Why can't it be both?"

"Forget it! Okay? Just forget it!"

"Hey . . . "

"What!"

"Don't worry," said Leskov in a tone of tender reassurance. "I already forgot."

Bennett flicked his cigarette into a puddle in the road, thrust his hands into his jacket pockets, and brooded sullenly.

After a while Leskov said, "We have to talk about this problem I got."

"What's the problem."

"It's a problem about two guys."

"I just told you I don't want you to talk about the play anymore, dammit."

"What play? I told you: I forgot the play! This is another problem. About another two guys."

"What's the problem."

"The problem is that these two guys, they don't know each other."

"So what about it."

"It bothers me."

"There are a lot of guys who don't know each other."

"I know."

"So what's the big deal."

"It drives me crazy."

"Why?"

"Because these two guys, they *ought* to know each other. If ever there were two guys who ought to know each other, it is these two guys."

"So introduce them."

"It's not so easy."

"Why? You're the big matchmaker, right?"

"Yeah. Well, see, I guess I'm not a very good matchmaker."

After a pause, Bennett said, "Who are the two guys."

"The two guys are you," said Leskov.

Bennett felt a chill of terror run up his spine.

"I don't know what you're talking about," he said.

Leskov kept silent.

"Look," said Bennett, and he touched Leskov gently on the arm and got him to stop walking, "you have got to be straight with me on this and tell me what the hell you mean by I am like two guys. It scares me!"

"Yeah? Well, it's a scary thing."

"What does it mean, dammit."

"It means that you were one guy last night, that you are another guy today, and that these two guys don't seem to know each other. And this is a big problem for me."

"Well, you are not so simple either, you know. In fact, you are one guy one day and another guy another day all the goddam time!"

"This is true. But these two guys that I am, they know each other. Do you ever get the feeling that these two guys that I am don't know each other? Tell me the truth."

"No," confessed Bennett uneasily.

"Well . . . so . . . see? It's, like, you don't remember . . . you know?"

"Yes," said Bennett.

"You do remember, though, don't you?"

"Of course."

"Then talk to me about it."

"You talk about it," said Bennett.

"That's not going to solve my problem, is it. I mean, I could talk about the guy you were last night, and I could talk about the guy you are today, but that is not going to tell me why the two guys don't seem to know each other, is it. Only you can tell me that."

"Talk about the guy I was last night," said Bennett resolutely, "and I'll tell you why the two guys don't seem to know each other."

Then, having second thoughts, he added hastily, "Wait . . . never mind . . . don't . . . don't tell me . . . "

104

"Why?" said Leskov in exasperation, as if all the irony had been drained out of him. "What the hell is going on with you!"

"Nothing . . . I just don't want you to . . . to talk about it . . . that's all!"

Leskov moved closer. "Tell me about the index cards," he said, peering intently into Bennett's eyes.

"What index cards?" said Bennett in alarm.

"The index cards you say you lost."

"I told you. They were lecture notes."

"Since when do you take lecture notes. In a year and a half I never saw you take notes in a classroom."

"I took some last week. In the novel course. You're not in the novel course."

"And you took notes on index cards."

"Yes."

"And you lost them."

"Yes."

"Where?"

"Just forget it, okay? Forget the damn index cards. I don't need them!"

"What's the last place we were at last night?" persisted Leskov.

"I said forget it!"

"Why?"

"Because I don't want to talk about it!"

"Why? Because you forgot? Because you forgot where you were last night?"

Bennett's heart began to beat rapidly, and he could feel the pulse in his throat. "No! Are you kidding? I remember everything perfectly!"

"Where were we last night."

105

"What are you, a detective?"

"I'm your friend."

"Then . . . then leave me alone!" Bennett waved his hands, as if warding off a swarm of flies, and started to walk away, stepping off the curb into the gutter, which was full of filthy rainwater that came up over his ankles and flooded his shoes.

Startled, he jumped back onto the curbstone.

"Damn!" Bennett stamped on the ground in a futile attempt to squeeze the water out of his shoes, making an absurd noise, something like the noise made by a wet mop when it is wrung.

"That does it," he said. "I'm going to get a flu. I always get a flu when I get my feet wet in the cold. Damn! Why don't I watch where I'm going? Damn! You're driving me crazy, you know?"

"I'm sorry."

"Forget it! It's not your fault!"

"Look, I . . . "

"Just forget it, forget it! Just don't talk to me anymore! Just . . . just . . . what the hell am I going to do? Damn! I . . . wait . . . wait, wait . . . I've got an idea . . . "

Bennett hurried over to a nearby tree, a large elm, and set his airline bag on the ground. At the same time he tilted his head to meet Leskov's eyes, which were staring at him now across a distance of about five yards with a helpless pained expression. As this pathetic scrutiny both confused and embarrassed him, he diverted his gaze at once and clenched his teeth in an effort to keep his mind on his feet; then he propped one shoulder against the tree, lifted his right

106

knee to untie the laces on his right shoe, and took the shoe off and also the sock. His other shoe and sock he took off in the same way. Dancing back and forth from one bare foot to the other on the cold wet cement, he squeezed some water out of the socks and stuffed them in the shoes. Then he squatted to open the airline bag and took out a flannel shirt, dry socks and sneakers. Then he propped one shoulder against the tree again, dried his feet with the flannel shirt, and put on the socks and sneakers. This done, he squatted a second time, to pack the flannel shirt back into the bag along with the wet shoes, then pressed his hands against his knees, pushing himself upright, and sighed in relief.

Just then, in the light cast on the ground by a streetlamp, he saw a shadow approaching, and he looked up to discover Leskov, not an arm's length away, bent forward at the waist, in an attitude that was undeniably ominous, in that it resembled the attitude he had assumed a short while ago as a prelude to the uppercut, except that now he did not swing his arm back like a bowler; instead, he knelt on one knee, then two knees, and, bowing his head close to Bennett's sneakers, began to tie the laces.

Astonished, Bennett stood still, scarcely daring to breath.

After Leskov had tied the laces of each sneaker in a double knot, he got back on his feet again with some effort.

"You didn't have to do that!" said Bennett. "Why did you do that?"

Leskov cast his eyes down. "I don't know, David," he said.

107

Then he put his hands into the pockets of his overcoat and, after a nod of the head, walked off down the street, conveying by the sheer force of his mood, which had suddenly become grave and forbidding, that he wanted, now, to be alone; and therefore, Bennett did not dare to follow.

The farther Leskov receded into the distance, the more he seemed like only a hat and an overcoat bobbing in the mist.

At the far corner he vanished.

Bennett gazed at the deserted street a few moments; then, deciding to call it a night, he picked up his airline bag and walked off in the opposite direction.

He walked quickly, making sure to leap over the puddles at the curbs.

It took him nearly an hour to get home, and when he arrived, he found Jimmy Fisher's Plymouth parked at the foot of the driveway.

FISHER AND BENNETT IN THE PLYMOUTH

The exits of Jimmy Fisher, even the routine exits of an ordinary day, leaving a classroom, a luncheonette, a party, were habitually tentative and tormented, as if he were forever engaged in an irresistable, active meditation on the hard truth that his going from one place to another altered the order of things irrevocably; therefore his surprise reappearance in town, only hours after he was supposed to have left for good, was perfectly characteristic, and Bennett could not help but smile.

He went over to the Plymouth and, resting both hands on the roof, ducked his head to the window.

"Come inside," he said. "I'll make some coffee."

Fisher leaned across the seat to release the lock on the door.

"Let's go for a drive," he said. "I want to talk."

"We can talk inside."

"I've left Olive."

"I know. She turned up at Leskov's a couple of hours ago, and I was there."

"Is she all right?"

"Come in the house. There's coffee, and there's wine. There are even some donuts."

"Better not. Olive has this weird ESP thing with me that she acts on all the time, and if she gets a hunch that I'm with you, she'll be here in a flash. I'll feel easier if we talk in the car. Is she all right?"

"She's in a lot of pain."

Fisher appeared to stop breathing, and his eyes, ordinarily lively, became fixed and dull.

Venetian blinds clattered somewhere. Bennett turned his head and saw his landlady standing at her living-room window. The room behind her was dark, but her face and her nightgown were lit by the glow of the streetlamp.

Bennett opened the door of the car and got in.

"Let's go," he said.

Fisher drove impatiently across a few hundred yards of suburban streets and then onto an old two-lane highway.

"This goes east to nowhere," said Bennett.

"It's easier to talk on the highway. I don't have to think about the road so much."

"Why don't you pull over, and we can talk standing still."

110

"I'd rather keep moving."

Suddenly the windshield glared, and Fisher squinted and violently stamped on the floor several times with his left foot to blink his lights at a truck, an enormous truck, that had its high beams on and had just loomed up out of a dip in the road.

"Goddam that son of a bitch!" he said, as the truck, with arrogant force, passed in a blinding, furious rush of light and air.

"That's the first time I ever heard you use language," said Bennett.

"So?"

"So it doesn't go with your face."

"Maybe if I keep at it," said Fisher, "my face will change."

The Devil and the Puppeteer

Fisher said, "I want to talk to you about your play. I came back over a hundred miles just to talk to you about it."

"You're kidding."

"I was halfway to the Vermont border tonight."

"You could've saved the gas and written me a letter."

"No, no, I had to talk to you tonight. Look, it was your play that made me decide to take off."

Bennett brooded for a moment. "Olive thinks it was Leskov who talked you into it," he said cautiously. "She thinks he's got, like, a hold on you."

"I know," said Fisher with irritation. "I know Olive thinks that Leskov has this so-called 'hold' on me. And I suppose he has. In a way. I mean, I'm fascinated. And I respect him. But the truth is that Leskov was against my splitting, and he tried to talk me out of it. I don't expect Olive to believe that, but it's the truth. Olive thinks that Leskov is some kind of a Svengali, and that he's got me hypnotized. Every time I open my mouth lately, she tells me that I sound like Leskov. And sometimes I guess I do. But not always. And anyway, so what! Who did I sound like before I sounded like Leskov? Tell me. I want to know who I sounded like!"

"Look, Fisher . . . "

"I sounded like my mother!"

"Look . . . "

"Anyway I don't imitate Leskov on purpose. It's something that just happens. I can't help it. I open my mouth, and Leskov jumps out. That's why I keep my mouth shut lately when he's around. I don't want him to catch me in the act. I'd feel as if he had something on me."

"Did Leskov really try to talk you out of splitting?"

"He was dead set against it. He talked about it all the time. And he made a terrific case. He laid it all out. All the comfort and security I'd be giving up. The working wife, the home, the whole bit."

"But he didn't convince you."

"Actually, I could never tell if he meant what he said. He always had this funny edge on his voice."

At this, Bennett ventured the opinion that perhaps Leskov had been playing devil's advocate.

Fisher thought for a moment in silence.

"You mean, Leskov has been pulling the strings all along," he said.

"No . . . "

"I'm just a puppet on a string. Is that what you're saying?"

"I didn't say he was playing puppeteer."

"No, you said devil's *ad*vocate," said Fisher, in a clumsy attempt at sarcasm, which missed its mark.

He ground his teeth and took in one quick noisy breath through his nose.

"Well, maybe," he added, suddenly looking very tired and sad.

The Traitor Revealed

They rode in silence for a while. Now and then a car passed. The night had grown cooler. On the left side of the road was a pine forest that stood in dark relief against a sky lit by three-quarters of the moon. On the right were uncultivated fields and some farmland and pastures. Here and there were small herds of cattle asleep on the grass, obscure figures that Bennett observed intently to see if he could detect, at such a distance and at such a speed, the rise and fall of their breathing.

Fisher broke the silence tentatively.

"Do you know what the truth is?"

Bennett turned his head and raised an eyebrow.

"The truth," continued Fisher, "is that it was your play that decided me."

"Before you talk about the play," said Bennett, "can I ask you a touchy question? Are you in love with someone?"

"You mean someone beside Olive."

"Yes."

"Look," said Fisher, "I'm going to tell you something."

With this promise, he lapsed into silence again.

After a minute or so had passed, Bennett said, "I think I know what you were about to say."

"You do?"

"I think so. Something about you and a guy in New Hampshire. Right?"

"How do you know about that!"

"I just know, that's all. And if I pretend that I don't, and you start talking about it, I'll feel like a clown."

There was a pause, during which Fisher shook his head from side to side several times and muttered to himself.

"Leskov told you," he said at last, with bitter certainty.

Bennett was embarrassed. "It won't go any further, I swear," he said.

"Don't swear."

"Look . . ."

"I mean it!" cried Fisher defiantly and on the verge of tears. "Tell anybody you like! After tonight I'm going to make a clean sweep anyway. All the sneaking around has got me down, and I'm just exhausted from it! I wish Leskov hadn't told you, though. Not that it really matters. In fact, I'm even glad that you know.

It's just that I'm disappointed somehow. Leskov swore that he wouldn't tell a soul and I believed him."

"Just to set the record straight, Leskov didn't tell me the story like he was passing on a juicy bit of gossip. I'd feel rotten if you held a grudge against him. He made me swear never to let on to you that he told me, and I guess I blew it."

"I won't hold a grudge."

"Also, I'd appreciate it if . . . "

"If what?"

"If the whole business came to an end right here."

Fisher sneered. "You mean, you don't want me to tell Leskov that you told me that he told you what I told him not to tell anybody."

"Yes."

The Where

Fisher said, "Don't worry about it. I was going to tell you anyway. Only first I was going to tell you about the play, and how it knocked me out, and how it made me decide right there, right after the final curtain, while you and the other actors were taking the curtain calls, that I had to go, and that I had to go right away, tonight, not tomorrow or the day after."

"But . . . you've come back. I'm sorry, Fisher, but I can't help but notice that you have come back."

"Not to Olive."

"True, but . . . "

"What?"

"Never mind. Where are you headed? New Hampshire? To see your . . . your friend?"

"Yes."

"And you're not coming back here?"

"No. That's it. I'm gone."

"Do you really think that's a good idea? I can understand your leaving Olive, but why give up school too? I wouldn't like to have written a play that was responsible for consigning you to a second-rate job or the unemployment lines. Besides, I heard you were doing really terrific in the science program. I even heard that the old guy who runs the biology labs made a big deal out of you once in front of the whole class and called you 'a perspicacious intelligence.' "

Fisher blushed. "Yes. That's right. Perspicacious. Brother."

"What's the matter? You don't seem pleased."

"I am absolutely thrilled. A lot of the guys in that lab now call me Perspicacious. Every time I run into one of them outside class, it's, 'Hi, Perspicacious,' or, 'Here comes Perspicacious.' It's not much fun. I have a hard enough time as it is . . . with this . . . this face of mine and . . . and . . . forget it. Poor old Bradley, he meant well, and, honestly, at the time he made the remark, I took it as an honor. He was a name in genetics once, and he knows his business. I just wish he'd paid me the compliment in private."

"Poor old Bradley is the old guy who is the head of the biology lab?"

"Yes."

"And what does poor old Bradley think of you and your perspicacious intelligence leaving school?"

"He's helping me out. He fixed it so I could write a couple of papers and a report on a few experiments and get credit for the semester. I don't need a lab for the experiments, just my microscope and also some reference material he lent me."

"I don't get this, Fisher. If you're leaving school, why do you care if you get credit for the semester or not?"

"I'm not leaving school. I'm leaving this school. You see, a couple of weeks ago, I received notice that, thanks to Bradley, I got a fellowship at McGill. Starting next fall."

"McGill! Great! Jesus, that's great, Fisher. Really, that's great! Congratulations."

Fisher blushed again. "Thanks," he said.

"Now this whole thing is starting to make sense to me!"

"To me too. My plan is to go to New Hampshire, spend a few weeks there with my friend, and then go to Montreal and try to get my friend to move up there with me. I know a few people in Canada. I have some family up there, a few cousins, an aunt and an uncle, and I think they can help me find a job to see me through until September. It's going to be fine. Really. Fine."

"It sounds good."

"It does, doesn't it. I can't believe I've been hesitating. If I hadn't gone to see your play tonight, honestly, I think I might have sat around and tortured myself for another six months."

"I don't get it. You have really got to explain this to me. I just don't see any connection between all this and my play."

117

"It's very simple. Your play is focussed mainly on the conflict between the two brothers, isn't it. The younger brother is a passionate man of action, and the elder brother is something else. Exactly what he is, I don't know. But he's not a man of action, that's clear, and in any case, he is pathetic, and every time he appeared on the stage, I wanted to run up there and strangle him. But the younger brother, he is wonderful. Even though everything he does leads him further and further into disaster, you can't help but admire him. Even there, in the cell, at the end, when he finds out that the family had not burned the village after all, and that he had unwittingly been the cause of their downfall, you can't help but admire him, because at least he acted, and he acted forcefully, and out of some deep, moral passion. Am I making any sense?"

"Well . . . yes . . . in fact, what you are saying is something like what Leskov said."

"Really?"

"Only he puts it more succinctly. He said that it is a play about two guys. One guy sits, and the other guy moves."

Fisher laughed. "That is pure Leskov. Is that all he said about it?"

"He said that the great stroke was when the guy who sits gets up."

Fisher laughed again, and his eyes lit up. "Great," he said.

"Then he said . . . " Here Bennett did an exaggerated imitation of Leskov's voice and manner: " 'He

118

gets up, see, but it's too late. He's been sitting too long. And the first move he makes, it's a clumsy one, a catastrophe.' "

Fisher wrinkled his nose in disapproval and looked troubled.

"I don't see it like that," he said.

"You take this seriously?"

"Yes. I don't see it that the elder brother, 'the guy who sits,' makes a clumsy move. I see it that he makes a graceful move, and that he makes it perfectly. I see it that he makes a move that guarantees absolutely that he will never have to move again, a move that will allow him to sit, once and for all, in eternity."

"Jesus, Fisher . . . "

"Anyway, can you see now why the play decided me?"

"Yes."

"And then the bit about the lovers going to Canada, that was like magic . . . for me. I even thought that maybe you were deliberately trying to send me a message."

"If you want to know the truth, Fisher, I hadn't even been thinking about you when I wrote that bit about the lovers going off to Canada."

"How can you be so sure? After all, I was born in Canada, and God knows I've talked to you about Canada often enough."

"I know, but . . . well, you had never talked to me about running off to Canada with a lover, for godsakes. Whenever you talked about Canada, it usually had something to do with either your father or the death of your father."

"That's not true. I talked about all sorts of things."

"Yes, but they were always things you saw or did with your father."

"That's not true either."

"Maybe not, but that's how I remember it. Maybe I remember it that way because when you talked about things you saw and did with your father, you talked more intensely, and so those are the things I remember. If I were to take an association test, and the tester were to say Canada, you know what my first response would be? Fisher's father."

"Then how can you say you weren't thinking about me when you wrote about Canada in your play, dammit!"

"Okay, okay. You have a point. Maybe I was thinking about you. But if I was, I swear I didn't know."

"How can you think about a thing and not know that you are thinking about it, for godsakes!"

"What the hell are you getting so angry about?"

"Nothing . . . nothing . . . sorry . . . " Fisher was suddenly quite morose, and he appeared to be gazing at rather than through the windshield.

The two friends fell silent for a minute or so.

Then Bennett said, "Answer a question for me. Where does my play take place?"

"Where? Somewhere in the . . . somewhere out West."

"Where out West? What state?"

Fisher deliberated for a moment.

"Montana?" he said anxiously.

The Mystery of the Other Cheek

Fisher took a Mounds candy bar from his jacket pocket and ripped the end of the wrapper with his teeth. He pushed one of the Mounds halfway out with his thumb and took a bite.

"Want some?" he said.

"Leskov socked me in the jaw tonight," said Bennett.

"What?"

"He socked me."

Fisher made a sign of amazement with the candy bar.

"You mean literally?" he said.

"Yes. Literally. With his fist. My jaw still aches."

"You're talking physically."

"Yes."

"You mean, he actually hit you. Physically. With his fist. Actually hit you in the jaw."

"Yes."

"Christ. But why?"

"I was going on at him and he got pissed off."

"Did you hit him back?"

"No."

"Good," said Fisher.

"Why is that good?" said Bennett, observing Fisher curiously.

Fisher glanced briefly at Bennett out of the corner of one eye and took another bite of the candy.

"How come you didn't hit him back?"

"I just didn't."

"I don't get it. He wouldn't stand a chance against you."

"He took me off guard, that's all."

"There is something you're not telling me," said Fisher.

"I get the same feeling about you."

"Maybe the thing you're not telling me and the thing I'm not telling you are the same thing."

"Maybe they are," said Bennett.

"So tell me."

"You tell me."

"I asked you first."

"Let's flip a coin." Bennett took a quarter from his pocket. He tossed it gingerly, caught it in his right hand and slapped it down on top of his left. "Call it."

"Heads."

Bennett exposed the coin. "It's tails."

Fisher put the last bit of candy into his mouth.

"Good," he said, crushing the wrapper into a ball and flinging it out the window. "Now I can get in on the act and be a traitorous pig-bastard like everybody else."

On the Distribution of a Secret

Fisher said, "Leskov is sick, and he doesn't have long to live. He has a very high-class disease."

There was a pause.

"Go ahead," said Bennett.

"What do you mean 'Go ahead!' Talk, dammit! Is that the reason you didn't hit him back, or isn't it!"

122

"That's the reason," said Bennett. "Ever since Leskov told me about the death bit, I've been very cautious with him. I always think of him now as more fragile than the rest of us . . . more temporary . . . and, somehow, for me, this gives him certain privileges. Do you know the name of the disease?"

"No," said Fisher. "Do you?"

"He wouldn't say."

"When did he tell you about it?"

"Last spring. In April. When did he tell you?"

"In May," said Fisher with sullen indignation. "And he told me that he hadn't told another soul, dammit, and that I was the only one in the world that he could trust. Christ."

"He told me the same thing. Did he tell you how many years the doctor gave him?"

"Two at the outside," said Fisher, "but less if he doesn't quit smoking."

Bennett said that Leskov told him the same thing, and Fisher appeared to be at once pleased and annoyed with the consistency in the two stories.

"I wonder if he told anyone beside you and me," he said.

"I think maybe he told Sarah. Tonight, after he hit me, Sarah got upset, and she started to come to me, like she wanted to comfort me . . . or apologize for him . . . whatever . . . and Leskov stopped her. He gave her a look and said, 'Let it alone. He knows.' And that wrapped it up. Sarah gave in, and that was that. They went back in the house together and left me sitting on the grass like an idiot. 'He knows!' Well, what else could that have meant except, 'He knows

123

I'm going to die.' So, I figured, well, okay, it's perfectly natural that he would tell his wife a thing like that, and maybe when he told me that no one else knew, he just assumed I would take it for granted that he didn't mean he hadn't told Sarah. But, somehow, it bugged me. Because all along I thought that I was the only one who knew. But then I started thinking that maybe a lot of people knew. I mean, people who are intimate with him and under his thumb. And I started to get this weird picture of a crowd, a small crowd of people, each of whom believes that he or she is the only one who knows this so-called secret. You see? I mean, I got this really weird picture!"

"Jesus, maybe the picture is true," said Fisher in a hushed voice, his eyes dancing with intrigue.

The Tears Behind the Veil of the Encyclopedia's Bride

Fisher said, "Who else do you think knows?"
Bennett kept silent.
"What about Orbach?" urged Fisher.
"I don't think the death routine would work on Orbach. He's, like, so cold."
"That's a cover-up," said Fisher.
"For what?"
"Schmaltz. Like one time I was up at his apartment with one of his roommates . . . the swishy one who works part-time in the library . . . you know him . . . Vernon. And Orbach and this other guy . . .

124

the little guy who lives there? . . . the music major with the red ears who always carries a clipboard?"

"Freddy."

"Right. Freddy. Orbach and Freddy were sitting in the livingroom, and Freddy had the M volume of the *The Encyclopedia Britannica* on his lap, and he was asking Orbach questions."

"You're making that up," said Bennett sternly.

"No. I swear. Freddy would ask Orbach a question about something in the encyclopedia, and if Orbach didn't know the answer, Freddy would tell him, but usually Orbach would know. I'd say he got about three out of four. The guy is really scary."

"Leskov mentioned something tonight about Orbach being married to the encyclopedia, but I thought it was just a joke."

"It's no joke," said Fisher. "The fantastic part is that while this quiz-kid thing was going on with Freddy and the encyclopedia, the hi-fi was playing *Wozzeck* on four speakers. Really loud. Deafening. Do you know *Wozzeck?*"

"No."

"It is a neoromantic, twelve-tone opera that sometimes has a tune to it and could tear your stomach out."

Bennett laughed. "And Orbach goes for that kind of thing . . . ?"

"I saw it with my own eyes. There he was, see, answering these encyclopedia-type questions—about margarine, for godsakes!—and at the same time he had his eyes closed, and the back of his head was against the wall, and his right hand was moving a little in time to this *Wozzeck* thing like a symphony conductor, and he looked like he was in some kind of ecstacy, and there was a tear, I swear to God, a real tear dripping out of his eye! That was the night I learned that margarine was invented by a guy named Mege Mauries in France in 1848 during the war."

"So what you're saying is that Orbach has a soft spot, and that Leskov must have got to it."

"Yes," said Fisher in extreme agitation, as if his whole being were rushing toward some terrific conclusion, "but he must have got to it with something heavy. Something like *Wozzeck,* see, or a fatal disease. Look, Orbach is working like a dog on all of Leskov's papers, and I can't see how else Leskov managed to enlist all that energy, can you? Orbach won't give anybody else the time of day. A couple of weeks ago I met him in front of the bookstore. Feckler's paperback place. 'Hi, Orbach,' I say, but he just keeps walking, and he puts up one hand like a traffic cop. 'I see you, Jimmy,' he says, 'but I'm following a thought, and I can't stop to talk.' Do you believe it? He's following a thought! And he just keeps walking! I swear to God! So, look, if I can't get Orbach even to stop and give me half a minute on the street, how did Leskov manage? Orbach will drop everything and dance to any tune that Leskov calls. I've seen it, believe me. Leskov has him translating Kant and proofreading and even doing research on the microfilm machines. This has been going on since the end of September. It's incredible. Freddy says he can't figure it out."

The abrupt mention of Freddy at this point, some-how, struck both Fisher and Bennett as comic, and they burst out laughing.

The Sitter

Bennett said, "What about Alice?"

The mention of Alice, at the moment, also struck the two young men as comic, and again they burst out laughing.

When they calmed down, Fisher said, "I don't know what to think about Alice. What do you think?"

"I don't know what to think either," said Bennett. "But she's such an easy mark that I don't think he'd have to go to such an extreme with her. On the other hand, he has her babysitting for him three and four nights a week for free, and that seems a lot to ask, even from Alice."

The Room in the Back of the Time Machine

An air of conspiratorial excitement was brewing between the two young men in the Plymouth, and they began to talk faster and with more spirit.

Fisher said, "Do you know who I think he must have conned? Feckler."

"Yes," said Bennett, lowering his voice, as if he were afraid of being overheard. "Definitely. Absolutely.

Feckler! Christ, he's such a bastard, that Feckler. One time he actually rapped my knuckles after I put a book back in the wrong place. And Leskov has him eating out of his hand! Feckler even has a room set up for him in the back of the store. Did you know that? About the room?"

"Sure," boasted Fisher. "Leskov invites me in there for coffee all the time."

"I never did understand that," said Bennett. "How come Feckler set up a room for Leskov? What the hell does Leskov need a room in the back of the bookstore for?"

"He goes back there to read and kibbitz with Feckler. Feckler eats it up. They talk about novels. Feckler is a big Truman Capote fan. *Breakfast at Tiffany's,* according to Feckler, is superior to both *Anna Karenina* and *Madame Bovary.* And Leskov, you should hear him, he actually encourages Feckler in this bullshit. One day, as we were leaving the store, I said to Leskov, 'How come you encourage Feckler like that? You don't really believe that crap, do you?' "

"And what did he say?"

"He laughed. 'Fisher,' he said, 'what we have here in this Feckler is a precious commodity and a first-rate buffoon out of the eighteenth century.' And then he said that he would never attempt to contradict Feckler, because Feckler is in a different time-warp, and in order to get Feckler to understand the argument, it would have to be translated into back-alley Restoration English and put in a time-capsule that could travel backward, and frankly he, Leskov, was at the moment technically underequipped for the job."

"I still don't understand what he needs the room for," said Bennett with annoyance. "At bottom he must be bored to tears by Feckler."

"Feckler brings him coffee. Really waits on him hand and foot. Brings him books and writing paper and Kleenex for his glasses. At first I used to think that all this was just an elaborate con to get Leskov to buy a lot of books. Which, by the way, he does. I know for a fact that he has bought over two hundred quality paperbacks just since the summer. I saw the bill. I also know, though, that he hasn't paid this bill yet."

"Do you think he will?"

"Who knows!" cried Fisher, letting go of the steering wheel and showing both his palms.

Then he gripped the wheel again.

"Anyway," he continued, "the reason I think Leskov likes this room is because when he's in it, it looks like he owns the store. He always leaves the door open, you know, so that when you go in to shop, you look in the back, and you see Leskov with his feet up on the desk, and Feckler running in and out with coffee and books and writing paper and messages and God knows what. And God forbid if Leskov doesn't come around for a few days! Feckler feels insulted! Really hurt! It's incredible."

"So you think he told Feckler too," said Bennett introspectively.

"What do you think?"

"You seem to be making a case for it."

"It's not so hard."

"I know," said Bennett, humorlessly stroking his chin like a detective in a melodrama. "We could probably make the case that he has told a lot of people in the thesis class as well."

"At least half," put in Fisher at once. "He has at least half of them on one kind of a string or another. Jesus, this is incredible!"

Fisher glanced to the right, apparently eager to have Bennett continue the line of argument, but Bennett was preoccupied.

"So, now what?" urged Fisher.

"What do you mean?"

"I mean, what do we do? We can't go around asking everybody if Leskov told them he has a fatal disease!"

"You can't," said Bennett. "Because you're leaving. But I can."

"You wouldn't."

"Why not?"

Doubtful Maternity

An air of gloom descended on the two young men, and they kept silent for a few minutes.

"Do you think he told Annie?" said Bennett at last, in a brooding, troubled tone.

The question took Fisher by surprise. "His daughter?" he said. "Jesus Christ, she's only a little kid!"

"So what?"

"You know, of course," said Fisher uneasily, "that Annie is not Sarah's child. Did you know that?"

"Are you serious?"

"Annie is a child by another marriage. Leskov's first wife."

130

"How do you know?"

"Leskov told me."

"He was lying," said Bennett with disgust and exasperation. "Just last week I heard Sarah telling someone on the telephone about how difficult her labor was. She said she was screaming in the labor room for ten hours. I heard her. I heard her talking about it on the phone!"

"Who would she be telling that to?"

"I don't know. What's the difference?"

"Maybe she lost the baby. Did she say it was Annie?"

"I just assumed."

"Oh, you assumed," said Fisher sarcastically.

"Look, Fisher, Leskov was lying!"

"Why would he lie about a thing like that?"

"Why does he lie to Feckler about *Breakfast at Tiffany's?* It's some kind of a power-play, that's all."

"Power over what?"

"I don't know! Everything!" Bennett was furious and literally trembling with indignation.

After a minute or so had passed, Fisher said, "I've never seen you like this."

"Like what?"

"This."

"What are you talking about, Fisher?"

"You're so . . . so . . . I don't know . . . I can't put my finger on it, but there is something strange in the way you . . . Is there something that you're not telling me?"

"Like what?"

"Like anything. Something important."

"Why are you saying this? What did I do that was so strange?"

"Nothing."

After a pause, Bennett said, "I'm going to tell you something, but you're not going to believe it."

"Try me."

"Leskov tied my shoelaces tonight."

Fisher wrinkled his brow slightly and kept silent.

"He got down on his knees," continued Bennett, "and tied my shoelaces! Do you believe that? He got on his knees on the ground, right on the wet sidewalk, and tied my shoelaces!"

Fisher laughed.

"No wonder you're acting so . . . so . . . he has really got you confused, right? First he ties your shoelaces, and then he socks you in the jaw! Jesus."

"No. It was the other way around. The sock in the jaw came first. He didn't tie the laces until about twenty minutes later."

"I thought you said that after he socked you, he went back in the house and left you sitting on the grass."

"That's right. But then I got up and knocked on the door, because I'd left my bag in his apartment . . . and he came out . . . he brought the bag out to me . . . you see? . . .and . . . and we went for a walk . . . and we had a talk . . . "

"About what? Did he apologize?"

"No . . . well, not directly . . . "

"So what the hell did you talk about?"

"Mainly about the play. And also about last night."

"You mean, about when you and he went to Smitty's."

"How do you know we went to Smitty's?"

"He told me."

"What else did he tell you?"

"Nothing," said Fisher. "He just told me you and he went to Smitty's and had a few drinks."

"You're lying."

"I am? Why? Is there something to tell?"

"Smitty's wasn't the only place we went to last night. We went to a few places."

"Really?" said Fisher with transparent insincerity. "He didn't tell me that. He only told me about Smitty's."

"What did he tell you about Smitty's?"

"That you went there."

"That's all?"

"Yes . . . but, look, can we drop this thing about Smitty's for a minute? How come Leskov tied your shoelaces?"

"I don't know!"

"But . . . what were your shoelaces doing untied in the first place?"

"I had just put on my shoes . . . or, rather, my sneakers."

"I thought you said you were out walking in the street."

"We were. But I had stepped in a puddle, and my shoes got wet, and I had dry sneakers in my bag, and so I decided to put them on, because whenever I get my feet wet, I always get sick."

"How did you manage to step in a puddle?"

"I wasn't looking where I was going. Leskov was getting me all worked up, and I just wasn't looking where I was going! And I stepped in a puddle!"

133

"What was he saying that got you so worked up?"

"He . . . he . . . I . . . I don't remember! What's the difference! The main thing is that this was a really strange thing for him to do! Don't you agree that this was a really strange thing for him to do?"

"I don't know. I wasn't there. Maybe this was just his way of apologizing for the sock in the jaw."

"Maybe it was, but it didn't feel like an apology."

"What did it feel like?"

"It was weird, Fisher. Really weird! When he started to get on his knees, at first I thought he was going to take a swing at me again."

"But he didn't, did he."

"No, but . . . "

"Then why was it so weird?"

"Because . . . because that's just not the sort of thing that you would expect one grown man to do for another . . . do you understand? It was more like something your mother might do for you when you're three years old."

"Did your mother do that for you?"

"What kind of a question is that! I don't remember anything at all that my mother did for me when I was three years old . . . do you?"

"No. All I know about those days is what she has told me."

"So? Do you think I'm any different from you in that respect? I don't remember either! I can tell you this much, though. While I can reasonably assume that my mother must have tied my shoelaces a considerable number of times when I was three, I can't imagine that she would ever have got down on her knees on a cold wet sidewalk in the middle of the night! . . . unless . . . "

"Unless what?"

"Unless it were a matter of life or death."

The Stowaway

Fisher narrowed his eyes, and a dark smile crossed his face.

"Listen to me," he said in a haunted, Leskovian voice. "I've got something . . . something interesting to tell you."

Bennett observed his friend suspiciously. "About what?"

Fisher stole a furtive glance at the rearview mirror. "Relax," he said.

"What's up?" said Bennett uneasily.

"You really want to know?"

"Yes, dammit, what's going on?"

"Well . . . " Again Fisher glanced at the rearview mirror.

"Well, what!" Bennett felt a chill across his arms and the back of his neck.

"Can I ask you a question first?"

"Just get on with it. You look so weird!"

"Well," said Fisher almost in a whisper, "what if you were suddenly to discover that, at this very moment, Leskov were hiding in the back seat."

Involuntarily Bennett widened his eyes. He glanced over his left shoulder, then his right, noted again the knowing smile on Fisher's lips, and at last let himself go and panicked. In a clumsy fit he twisted himself around and stood on his knees on the seat, craning his neck to examine the floor in the rear.

At this, Fisher laughed, howling pitilessly, even as a blow from Bennett's fist knocked him against the door, and the car swerved into the oncoming lane.

Smoke without Fire

"You could have got us killed!" said Fisher, commanding the road again and rubbing his right shoulder.

Bennett folded his arms across his chest and glowered.

Fisher smiled. "What if there had been traffic?" he said.

Bennett kept silent. He lit a cigarette and smoked. When he was done, he crushed the burning ash under his foot and flicked the stub out the window.

Then he asked Fisher a question: Why were they both afraid of Leskov?

In response, Fisher made a show of bewilderment, conceding that he, of course, was a *little* afraid, but . . .

"But not as afraid as I am," interrupted Bennett sarcastically.

"I didn't say that," said Fisher.

"But that's what you meant."

"Well, after all, it's not me that jumped out of my seat a couple of minutes ago."

"I didn't jump. I just turned around."

136

"You almost went through the roof."

"If I ever pulled a trick like that on you, you would wet your pants."

Fisher laughed.

"Maybe," he conceded.

"So answer! Why are we so afraid? If you had hinted that Orbach, or Feckler, or Alice, or anybody else we've been talking about, was hiding in the back seat, I guess I would have been surprised and embarrassed, but not so . . . so scared! Do you see? Not so scared!"

"That's Leskov, that's all," said Fisher, attempting to lighten the tone. "He has those haunted eyes, and there is something about him that scares people. Olive once told me that the first time she met him, her knees shook, and she got a spasm in her throat. Like an idiot I suggested that probably it was just some kind of animal-magnetism thing, and she blew her stack. In fact, she said that that was precisely the point."

"What was?"

"That there was no animal thing, no animal feeling at all. And that was what had scared her."

"Did you believe her?" said Bennett with intense interest.

"I believe that she felt what she said she felt," said Fisher with a subtle smile and a peculiar look in his eye. "Myself, of course, I don't read him that way."

Bennett observed his friend with curiosity. "How do you read him?"

"I told you."

"He's just scary."

"Right. He has a certain quality, that's all. Like bad breath. Of course he cultivates it. He has it, he knows it, and he cultivates it."

"He eats raw onions," offered Bennett.

Fisher gave a short laugh. "Like that," he said, in a calculated imitation of Leskov, slicing the air decisively with his open hand, to signify that he wanted to dismiss the subject.

The Logic and the Gun

Fisher said, "You know Leskov's logic class?"

"What about it?"

"He punched one of the students in there."

"In class?"

"In front of the blackboard. Last semester."

"Who told you that?"

"Leskov."

"He was lying," said Bennett.

"How do you know?"

"It would have been all over the school, and he would have been canned on the spot."

"He punched you, didn't he?"

"So what?"

"Is it going to be all over the school?"

"He didn't punch me in a classroom."

"True."

"It's different," insisted Bennett.

"All right. Forget it."

"I will. Did you ever sit in on that class?"

"It's a freshman course."

"So what?"

"So I had that junk five years ago, and I hated it. Why do you ask?"

"There was a woman in that class," said Bennett. "An older woman. A kind of Madame Bovary type. In her forties. I was just wondering if you knew her, or if Leskov ever told you about her."

"The one that fell for him?"

"Yes."

"Orbach mentioned her a couple of times," said Fisher. "Also I saw her once having coffee with Leskov in the luncheonette. She was really coming on. Like Shirley Temple style, with the fluttery eyes and the giggles and the whole ensemble."

"That's the one."

"What about her? Did Leskov have it off with her?"

"You don't know the story?"

"No."

"You didn't hear about the scene with the husband?"

"She had a husband?"

"You never heard about this?"

"No, dammit," said Fisher in exasperation.

"Well . . . the husband turned up after class one night . . . "

"Wait. Who told you about this?"

"Leskov. The husband turns up, and he says he wants to have a talk. 'A civilized talk.' Then he shuts the door and makes a speech."

"Wait. Is the wife in the room?"

"Yes. The wife is in the room. 'I know how my wife feels about you,' says the husband, 'and it's absolutely all right with me if she has an affair with you, just as long as she understands that, in the end, she will have to pay the piper.' "

"What happened?"

"Leskov announced that he owned a gun, and that in the future he would take it to class. 'And if I ever see your face around here again,' he says, 'I'm gonna blow your brains out.' "

"And?"

"The guy never showed up again."

"What about the woman?"

"She got a 'C' in the course."

The two friends kept silent for a minute or two. Then Fisher, apparently quite troubled, asked Bennett if he thought the story were true.

"I don't know," said Bennett. " 'Pay the piper,' though, was the slogan of the day. Every ten minutes or so Leskov would repeat it out of the blue. 'Pay the piper.' Like that. In this very cynical, creaky voice, with a gruesome look on his face."

"Do you think he really owns a gun?"

"If he does, I never saw it."

"Do you think he would actually have shot the guy if he had turned up again?"

"I don't know!" said Bennett. "That's the whole point! Don't you see? It's like you just said. He has this scary thing . . . this 'quality' . . . and he plays on it . . . cultivates it. Just look at you and me. He really has us cooking, right? Like: Maybe he owns a gun, but maybe he doesn't. And maybe he would have shot the guy, but maybe not; maybe he just said it to scare him, or maybe he never even said it at all!

Maybe he just *said* that he said it . . . to . . . to scare *me!* Get it? It's all maybes. Maybes and threats. That's the whole game. And to keep himself in business, all he has to do is hand out a rap on the jaw now and then, and Bingo, he has a going concern. Like, he hit Olive tonight with a lulu, and I thought she was going to drop dead on the spot."

Fisher paled, and he took his foot off the accelerator.

"What do you mean?" he said.

"I wasn't going to say anything," said Bennett nervously, after a pause.

"Leskov hit Olive?"

"I wasn't going to say anything."

"You keep saying that!"

"Sorry."

"Where did he hit her? Wait a second. He hit her?"

"Not physically. But he got her where it hurts."

"He said something."

"Right. He said something. I wasn't going to say anything."

"For chrissake, man, what did he say!"

"Put your foot back on the gas," said Bennett harshly. "You're doing fifteen miles an hour, and somebody may come around a curve and bust our ass."

Fisher hit the accelerator, and the car shot forward.

"Talk," he said.

The speedometer began to rise rapidly.

"Look," said Bennett in a nervous, conciliatory tone, "when Olive turned up at Leskov's tonight, she was in a state. Really steaming. She had this idea in her head that it was Leskov who broke up her marriage, and she looked like she was ready to kill him."

"Figures," said Fisher.

Bennett glanced at the speedometer. "Anyway," he said, "after a while, he managed to get her quiet and . . . "

"He got her quiet?"

"Yes."

"That's hard to believe."

"Maybe. But he did. He got her quiet. And then he said something nasty, and she ran out of the house. And that's the whole story. Alice went over to comfort her, though, so there's nothing to worry about."

With a grim look in his eye, Fisher pushed the accelerator to the floor and held it there.

"I want to know what he said."

"All right!" cried Bennett in terror, as the speedometer touched ninety. "Just slow down, and I'll tell you all about it!"

Fisher slowed down.

"Okay?" he said softly, once the speedometer had come down to forty-five.

"Okay," said Bennett, drawing a breath, his heart pounding in his throat.

Heidegger

Fisher said, "First tell me how he got her quiet."

"He brought out some suits, and he showed them to her."

"Suits?"

"Yes. On hangers."

"What for?"

"I don't know. It was absolutely off the wall. Here was Olive with murder in her eye, telling Leskov what a son of a bitch he is, and all of a sudden Leskov starts to talk about how much he paid for these suits! Like four hundred dollars apiece. And she just looked at him like he was crazy."

"And she shut up."

"Yes."

"Fantastic," said Fisher with an admiring nod, his eyes lighting up.

"Then he told her about your visit to Heshel Brustein," said Bennett.

"What for? I hardly said two words to Heshel."

"Leskov said that it really floored you when Heshel came out with that remark about Heidegger."

"That's true," said Fisher eagerly. "I'll never forget that. Leskov asked Heshel about Heidegger, and the old guy put his hand on Leskov's knee and said, 'Mister Leskov, let me tell you something. I shit on Heidegger.' It was far out."

"I don't understand. What's the big deal?"

"You had to be there. See, Heshel had already been talking for about an hour. And he talked like a book. A very good book. Very clean, pure. I never heard anything like it. And he had this very cultured European accent. Every word came at you like a bell in a tower. And then, then, all of a sudden, he makes this weird connection between excrement and Heidegger, and it just knocked me out, that's all. I don't know how to describe the impact it had on me. You had to see his face. A couple of days ago, I was talking to Orbach about it, and he filled in some of the gaps for me. According to Orbach, Heshel and Heidegger had been pretty tight in the twenties, but later, in the thirties, Heidegger turned into a yes-man under the Third Reich, and while he was holding down a cushy job at the University of Naziberg, Heshel was hanging out around the gas chambers, eating garbage out of the can."

There was a pause.

Then Bennett said, "Leskov didn't explain afterward?"

"Leskov is a prick. He never explains."

"Tell me about it," said Bennett, in a tone of despairing assent.

"But how did Olive take all this?" said Fisher. "Did she get it?"

"Do you?" said Bennett.

"I do now. But it took me three weeks to sort it out."

"So then what the hell are you asking me! Olive looked at him like he was from another planet!"

"He is," said Fisher with solemnity. "The guy is from another planet. A whole other solar system."

Denouement

Bennett said, "Olive was so confused by this time, that Leskov could do anything he wanted with her. So he kept throwing one damn crazy idea after another at her, and she just stood there, gaping at him and straining to make the connections, and straining quite desperately, too, because he had led her to believe, you see, that he was trying to explain why you left her."

"Was he?"

"Maybe."

"I explained it all myself."

"What did you tell her?"

Fisher shrugged his shoulders. "That I'm not cut out for married life," he said uneasily.

"That's it?"

"Basically."

"Great."

"It's the truth!"

"So is twelve apples in a dozen, Fisher, but that is not the kind of truth Olive needs from you."

"Yeah, I know. She's gotta have thirteen."

"She's in love with you, you idiot."

"All right! So I'll go back to her!"

"I'm not telling you to do that."

"Then what are you telling me?"

"I'm telling you she wants to know what the story is."

"The story is that I'm not cut out for married life."

"That's not a story."

"Then what is it?"

"It's not a story, that's all."

"Just skip it, dammit. What happened next?"

"Leskov got very affectionate and playful with her. He even made a few jokes."

"But she didn't fall for it, right?"

"Wrong. She warmed up to him like a little girl."

"Really?"

"Really. Then, after a while, she said something like, 'So what are you saying?' And Leskov smiled at her in this very fatherly way, and his voice got all nice and oily, and he said, 'What I'm saying is . . .' "

"Go ahead! Don't stop now!"

'What I'm saying is. . . that your husband is a cocksucker.' "

Fisher held his breath for a moment.

Then he said, "What did she do?"

"She ran out of the house."

"Christ."

What's Wrong with Alice?

Fisher said, "What is on his *mind* when he says things like that?"

"I don't know."

"Has he got a purpose, or is he just a natural-born son of a bitch?"

"I don't know."

"It's weird."

"What did you say?"

"I said, it's weird!" shouted Fisher angrily. Then, lowering his voice, he added, "Do you think Olive is all right?"

"Alice is with her."

"Oh, yeah, I forgot. Alice. Great."

"What's wrong with Alice?"

The Wandering Poker Game

Bennett said, "Did Leskov ever talk to you about Korea?"

"He told me that he punched a sergeant once and got a court-martial, but he never said much else."

"Did he see action?"

"You mean, did he fire a gun and kill anybody," said Fisher.

"Yes."

"I don't know. He never talks about it."

"I think he probably never saw action."

"Why?"

"I don't know," said Bennett. "Maybe he did. That would explain a few things anyway."

"Like what?"

"Like that look he gets in his eyes that says, 'I've been walking around the block for two thousand years, and I need a rest.' Did you know that he has had that Eugene Sue novel on his desk since last Christmas?"

"Which one?"

"*The Wandering Jew*," said Bennett. "And he is always bugging me to read it. I think he really identifies with him."

"With Eugene Sue?"

"The Wandering Jew."

"Don't be ridiculous," said Fisher. "Leskov doesn't identify with anybody, except maybe Phil Harris."

"Who is Phil Harris?"

"He's a singer. He used to be on the Jack Benny Show. He sings, 'Gonna see my dear ole mammy, she's fryin' eggs and boilin' hammy, and that's what I like about the South.' "

"Oh, him. I know that guy. Rough, deep voice. Like a boozer. He also does that song about the poker game and the one-eyed man."

"That's him."

"Leskov sings that poker song all the time," said Bennett with a scowl, then added, "I hate it."

The Road to Morocco

Bennett said, "A few months ago he tried to talk me into going to North Africa. Morocco."

"What for?"

"He said he knew people there, and that they would take care of me. He even wrote a letter to one of them, and he showed me the reply. I almost went."

"I don't get it. Why Morocco?"

"He hinted that I would learn something there that was important."

"Like what?"

"How should I know! At first I got paranoid about it, and I thought he was just trying to get rid of me."

"Why would he want to get rid of you?"

Bennett shrugged his shoulders and lowered his eyes. "I don't know," he said.

Fisher brooded for a moment, then said with irritation, "What the hell does he know about Morocco?"

"He lived there for a while. He was a disc jockey there."

"You're kidding."

"That's what he told me. He used to be a French disc jockey on a classical music radio program in Morocco."

"What's a French disc jockey?"

"He did the program in French."

"Do you believe it?" said Fisher.

"Do you?" said Bennett.

"His French is good. I heard it."

"That's not what I asked you."

"You saw the letter from Morocco?" asked Fisher.

"Yes."

"You saw the cancelled stamp on the envelope?"

"Yes."

"Then maybe I believe it. Why didn't you go?"

"Watch the road."

Mermaid in the Chamber

Bennett said, "Once he told me a story about a woman in Morocco. He said he lived with her in a house on the beach for six days, and on the seventh day he woke up in an empty bed, and there was a note on the table, and he never saw her again."

"What did the note say?"

"He didn't tell me."

There was a pause.

"So, what about it!" said Fisher in exasperation.

"So what about what?"

"What happened next?"

149

"I don't know. That's it."

"That's the whole story?"

"That's all he told me."

"What did she look like?"

"He never said."

"What nationality was she?"

"I had the feeling that she was a cosmopolitan type."

"Is that how he described her?"

"That's just my own idea," said Bennett.

"Was he in love with her?"

"I don't know."

"So, what's the point?"

"I'm not sure."

"So, why did he tell you about it?"

"He didn't actually tell me about it. He just mentioned it."

"So, why are you telling *me* about it?" said Fisher.

"It just popped into my mind, Fisher, because we were talking about Morocco . . . and . . . because . . . I think about it a lot."

"What's there to think! The bastard didn't tell you a single thing about it!"

"It was the tone. 'There was a woman in Morocco.' Like that. That's all he needs to say, and it sounds like he's in an RCA echo-chamber, and it sticks in your mind. And then the eyes, too. The eyes are saying, 'You and I, David, we both know that woman in Morocco.' And all of a sudden, there she is. I can see her as plain as day. And I think to myself, 'What the hell is going on here? Is this son of a bitch hypnotizing me, or what!' "

150

The Word

Bennett lit another cigarette and smoked.

He thought: If I could understand Leskov, maybe I could get to the bottom of what happened last night.

Why this should be the case, however, he had no idea.

He said, "One day, a couple of weeks ago, Leskov and I were in town, just hanging out, just the two of us, walking around, making jokes about this and that, very pleasant and friendly. Then, about two o'clock, we went into the luncheonette and had a coffee and a piece of pie, and when we leave, he says, let's cross the street, because he has to go to the hardware store for Sarah. So, just to make conversation while we're waiting for the traffic light to change, I ask him what he has to get, and he says, 'Like, something in a can.' And he says it with contempt. And he gives me a look, a really mean look, as if I'd offended him in some way, and his tone is so harsh and nasty and unexpected, that I'm shocked by it, and I can't talk for a couple of minutes. Also, I can't figure out if the contempt is for me, or for the 'something in a can,' or what.

"Anyway, we go into the store, Harrison's, and Leskov goes up to the counter and says that he wants to look at some lawn chairs. Now, lawn chairs is an expensive item with a big mark-up, and the guy behind the counter gets all excited. Do you know who I'm talking about? The big guy with the arms, who wears the white shoes and the green eyeshade."

"You mean Ira. That's Harrison's brother-in-law."

151

"Ira. That's it. So, Ira runs around the counter and takes us back to the lawn chairs and shows us four or five varieties. And Leskov, he makes a tremendous fuss. He sits in them and bounces up and down and even kicks one of them in the leg like it was a tire on a second-hand car. Finally, he says that he likes them all, and that he will take two of each.

"Well, the big guy, Ira, he starts to hyperventilate, and he whips a pad out of his back pocket, and he writes up the order. When he's done, he asks what is a convenient time for delivery, and Leskov says, 'Any time next week.' 'But we can send them right over, if you like,' says Ira. 'Better not,' says Leskov. 'The plumbers are coming to clean the septic tank in a few days, and the chairs will just get shit all over them.'

"Now, Ira, he doesn't know what to do with this remark, so he just gives Leskov a very nervous smile, and his face twitches a little, and he says something like, 'You're the boss,' or something like that, and then he walks us to the front and opens the door for us in this very obsequious way that could make you throw up, and right there Leskov stops. He stops and snaps his fingers and shuts his eyes. 'Something wrong?' says Ira. 'I almost forgot,' says Leskov, and he starts to chew his lip. And Ira just stands there, holding his breath, and he's probably thinking, 'Oh, God, maybe the guy doesn't want to buy the chairs after all.'

" 'Listen,' says Leskov finally, and he looks at Ira in this very penetrating way, 'you got any polyurethane?' Well Ira, he is so relieved, he almost busts a gut. 'Sure!' he says. 'I got polyurethane all over the place! How much do you need?' 'I need a quart,' says

Leskov. 'It's for my wife. She does furniture.' So we go back into the store, and Ira rushes over to the polyurethane. 'Do you want glossy or flat?' he says. 'Glossy,' says Leskov. 'Do you want Dupont or the discount brand?' 'Gimme the goddam Dupont,' says Leskov, and he reaches for his wallet. 'Never mind,' says Ira. 'I'll throw it in for nothing. Comes with the lawn chairs.' "

"And then Leskov calls back the next day and cancels the chairs, right?" said Fisher.

"No. He had Sarah call."

Fisher said, "Leskov likes to make a big production out of everything."

"You're missing the point," said Bennett.

"The only point is that Leskov wanted to get himself a free can of polyurethane, and that's all there is to it."

"He mailed Ira a check for the polyurethane right after Sarah called."

"Really?"

"Really."

"Then what was the point?"

"I have an idea about it," said Bennett.

Bennett said, "My idea is, that he just didn't want to say the word."

"Polyurethane."

"Yes."

"Are you trying to tell me that you believe that Leskov went through that whole song and dance about the lawn chairs, just so that he didn't have to say 'polyurethane?' "

"Yes," said Bennett.

"But he did in the end, right? You did say he turned around in the doorway and asked Ira straight out if he had any polyurethane. Didn't you say he said that?"

"Yes, but, see, that's different. By that time, it was only an afterthought. Look, it isn't just 'polyurethane.' It's 'glossy,' too, and 'Dupont.' Don't you know what I'm talking about? I mean, when he says words like that, he always has this . . . this . . . like . . . *tone!*"

Radiant and Holy and Blind

Fisher glanced at the clock on the dashboard and said, "We've been talking about Leskov for almost an hour."

"I know. It's important."

"Why?"

"Because he has us by the balls."

"Do you think so?"

"Yes. And we have to get to the bottom of it."

"Why?" said Fisher, somewhat bewildered, narrowing his eyes suspiciously.

"Because because, okay?" said Bennett with irritation and passionate intensity. "Look, either Leskov is just thumbing his nose at the universe, in which case he can go to hell, or else he has an idea, a vision, some kind of ground, in which case what is it? I mean, if Leskov has ground, why has he got to be so fishy about it? Like he has a new chapter in his thesis, and the title is *The Holy Kant,* which is an expression I've

154

heard him use a lot, sometimes with two 'holies,' and sometimes in German, but always with a sneer, and it really bugs me, because I can't ever figure out what he's getting at. Once I asked Orbach about it, and he said that some of Kant's admirers use that expression, but with sincerity, and this gets Leskov's goat and gives him heartburn. And so, when Leskov says, 'The Holy Kant,' with this sarcastic edge, that's what it's about, the admirers and the heartburn.

"At first I thought, 'Okay, maybe that's it.' But then, one day I was with Leskov at the luncheonette, and Jeffrey was there, and Violet, and Gregg, and Steinmetz, and Herby, the whole front-seat crowd from the thesis class, and Leskov was doing a number. Like on Kant's bit about, 'What if all men were to do as I do?' I don't remember what Leskov said exactly, but he made it look like the dumbest idea in the whole history of morals, and he cracked everybody up."

"You too?"

"No. I didn't think it was funny. In fact, neither did Leskov, I think, because at the end, while the others, especially Steinmetz, were falling all over themselves in this big hysterical ha-ha scene, Leskov turned to me and gave me this very just-between-the-two-of-us-type tragic look, and when the laughing stopped, he smiled and seemed kind of embarrassed and said, 'I guess I ought to be in vaudeville.' And then he started to push himself up out of his chair, very slow, like an invalid, and when he got halfway up, he said, 'I feel terrific,' and then he turned white, and he passed out."

"I heard about that," said Fisher. "And Steinmetz caught him, right?"

"Right. Steinmetz. He was like lightning. Then the waitress brought ammonia and a wet towel, and when Leskov came to, she got on her knees and put his head in her lap, and he said, 'I shouldn't have done that. What if everybody were to pass out? Who would put the pee-pee in my nose and wake me up?' But nobody laughed this time. And Steinmetz, I don't know why, but he seemed really irritated, and he just marched out of the luncheonette without paying his check."

"Who paid?"

"Leskov. Well, he put it on his account. Did you know that Leskov is the only one in town with a line of credit in the luncheonette? For me they wouldn't even cash a ten-cent refund check that I got from a bum call on a pay phone. Like this luncheonette won't trust the Bell Telephone Company for a lousy dime, but Leskov they give a line of credit to. Anyway, that day I started to think that Orbach may be off the mark about Leskov and Kant. Because why does Leskov make jokes about Kant and then pass out when people laugh at the punchlines?"

"Maybe the jokes and the passing-out don't have anything to do with each other," said Fisher.

"Maybe they don't. But it looks like they do. Doesn't it?"

"I wasn't there."

"So what!"

"Why are you getting so worked up?" said Fisher with icy disapproval.

"Because it drives me bats! Look, Fisher, I can't figure out if Leskov gives a damn about Kant or what. And that means the whole bit is just another one of his freaky ambiguities that I could live without. Like he took Annie out of nursery school last month and put her in another one. And when I asked him why he pulled her out of the first one, specially as she had said she liked it, Leskov said that he had liked it too, at first, but then one day he visited the class and the teacher turned him off. 'What's wrong with the teacher?' I said. And he said, 'She brings her lunch in a paper bag and keeps a thermos bottle on her desk.' Then he looks at me like he thinks I know exactly what he means, but I didn't! I didn't understand what the hell he was talking about!"

"So, what did you say?"

"I just let it drop. I figured, what's the use? I'd give my left nut, though, to find out what he really thinks about Kant."

"Have you ever read Kant?" said Fisher.

"No."

"Then what's the big deal?"

"It's just that one idea. It haunts me."

"Which idea?"

"The one about making moral decisions on the basis of the question, 'What if all men were to do as I do?' In the imperative it's classier: 'Act as if the maxim of thy action were to become by thy will a universal law of nature.' Now, I think that's pretty good. In fact, it's beautiful. And I can't see why Leskov is always carrying on about it. And I'd like to know his opinion! I mean, does he think it's a good idea, or doesn't he! And if he doesn't, why!"

157

"He thinks that it's infantile," said Fisher drily, "but he has complicated feelings about it."

Bennett looked at his friend in surprise. "How do you know?"

"I read the new chapter in manuscript. The whole thirty pages is about that one idea."

"The whole chapter?"

"Yes."

"Is it good?"

"I can't judge," said Fisher.

"What's it like?"

"It's weird. I copied down the last sentence. It's on the notepad in the glove compartment."

Bennett opened the glove compartment.

"It's on the last page," added Fisher.

> Kant writes like an angel,
> radiant and holy and blind,
> a species unto himself.

"What does it mean?" said Bennett.

"That's what I asked him. I was reading it on the sofa in his livingroom a few weeks ago, while he was wandering around the apartment. Every two minutes he'd come over and glance at the page I was on, and then he'd go away. When I finished, the first thing I did was read him the last sentence aloud and ask him the same thing you just asked me, 'What does it mean?' 'You read very nice,' he says. 'You ought to go on the stage.' 'Okay,' I say, 'but what does it mean!' And he says, 'It means, I gotta make caca.' Then he goes into the bathroom and shuts the door, and I hear him lift the cover on the toilet seat and bang it against the tank, and then he shouts, 'Go home, putz, and read Aquinas!' "

"So, what did you do?"

"I copied that sentence on the pad and went home."

"Did you read Aquinas?"

"I read a synopsis in Fuller's *History of Philosophy.*"

"Did it help?" said Bennett.

"Yes."

"Well?"

"You want to hear?"

"Go ahead."

Saint Thomas and the Angels

Fisher said, "I'll be Aquinas, and you be the dummy who asks questions. Ask me who is God."

"Who is God."

"God is perfect. He is absolutely good and absolutely simple. He is existence and essence all at once, and He is pure form. He is, forget about it, Unimaginable. Also, He is the First Cause. Ask me who we are."

"Who are we," said Bennett.

"You are not going to like this. We are not perfect. Also, we are not pure. We are form, and we are matter, and we are very particular. Ask me who angels are."

"Who are angels."

"Angels, too, are not perfect. However, they are pure. They are pure, but they are not perfect. Ask me pure what."

159

"Pure what."

"Pure form. Ask me why they are not perfect."

"Why."

"Because, if they were perfect, they would be God. Now we come to a problem. Ask me about it."

"What's the problem."

"Angels are different from one another. Ask me why that's a problem."

"Why."

"Because if they are different from one another, they are particular. Ask me so what."

"So what."

"If they are particular, they are not angels. Ask me why."

"Why."

"Angels are pure form. Ask me so what."

"So what."

"Pure form can't be particular. Ask me why."

"This is getting ridiculous."

"Just ask me."

"Can't you just explain the thing straight out?"

"No. I get confused. Just ask."

"I forget the question."

"Why can't pure form be particular."

"Okay, go ahead," said Bennett.

"Well, ask me!"

"Christ. *Why can't pure form be particular.*"

"Because Aquinas travels in the best circles."

"Wait. This time you don't have to tell me. I'll just go ahead and ask. What, Fisher, do you mean?"

"Actually, I don't need a question here," said Fisher.

"But I do, dammit. What the hell does that mean!"

160

"I thought it was pretty clear. It means just what it says. It means that in the circles Aquinas travels in, pure form is never particular. This is axiomatic, that's all. Okay?"

"Okay."

"Now, ask me how Aquinas settles it."

"Settles what?"

"Settles how angels can be different from one another and also not particular."

"Forget it," said Bennett. "He can't do it. If he does, he is just playing with words. If angels are different from one another, then they have to be particular. There is no way out."

"You, my friend, have a shallow mind. Also, you will never make a name for yourself in the Medieval Period."

"All right. How does he do it?"

"Ask me one more time."

"Are you kidding? Just tell me how he does it, for chrissake!"

"Okay. This is what he says. He says that each angel is a type, a whole species all by itself."

"A species," said Bennett, somewhat surprised, and with interest.

"Yes."

"A whole species."

"Yes. What do you think?"

"It's neat," said Bennett.

"Do you think so?"

"Yes. It's really neat. I like it."

"Maybe we could bottle it," said Fisher.

"Wait. So this means . . . this means that each angel is not a particular, but a universal . . . each

161

angel is the absolute type and the one and only member of a unique species . . . "

"Right."

"So the world of angels is like a Noah's ark."

"Right. Except that the angels don't go in two by two."

"They go one by one."

"Right," said Fisher. "And since they are strictly a formal crowd, they dance, but they never touch. They just light each other up."

"And Leskov is using this idea to say something about Kant."

"Yes."

"Leskov is saying that Kant is like one of these angels out of Saint Thomas."

"Yes. Well, that he writes like one of them, or . . . or that he writes as if he thinks he was one of them. But he's not, see? He is a man . . . or *was* a man . . . at one time . . . see?"

"Okay," said Bennett, and then he lowered his eyes and brooded for a few moments.

"What's wrong?" said Fisher.

Bennett looked up, as if waking from a dream.

"Do you get it?" he said with intense, child-like curiosity.

"Who needs it!" cried Fisher. "Sarah told me that she found Dimitri reading *The Metaphysics of Morals* at three a.m. in the kitchen a couple of weeks ago, and he was weeping. He had a cup of coffee in his hand, and the book in his lap, and the son of a bitch was weeping!"

By the Light of the Clock

The two friends fell silent, Fisher gazing at the windshield, Bennett at the notepad.

Again and again Bennett scanned Leskov's words in Fisher's hasty scrawl and tried to conceive in his mind's eye the image of an angel. For some while he contended for perfect clarity, but he could not get it. In the end he resorted to livelier means. From his jacket pocket he took a pencil and placed the notepad on his knees. Then he bowed his head to exploit the dim green light from the clock on the dashboard and began to draw. With his fingers twisted tightly around the pencil, he bore down with stern pressure, committing his first line in the space below Leskov's words.

First he drew a head, then a neck and shoulders, then wings, a halo, and dark glasses, then ears, then a straight inconspicuous nose and a smile, then feet, very tiny feet, and a gown. Then for several minutes he puzzled over the hands and arms, how to shape them and in what attitude. At last, in his most solemn stroke, he returned the pencil to his pocket and drew no arms or hands at all. Then he sat up straight to consider his work under a wider aspect—all in all, a flat figure, stylishly two-dimensional—nodded witlessly three times and, after tossing the pad back into the glove compartment, slammed the little door with the heel of his palm.

Fisher, who had been silent throughout Bennett's artistic exercise, was startled by the sound. He shook his head and blinked.

"Christ," he said.

"What's wrong?" said Bennett.

"I just realized that I've been driving blind for about ten minutes."

"What are you talking about?"

"I haven't been seeing the road."

"You've been driving all right," said Bennett reassuringly.

"I must have been driving in my sleep!"

"Do you want me to drive for a while?"

"No. I'm fine now."

"Come on. Let me drive."

"No," Fisher declared, and he set his jaw.

The Mystery of the Vanishing ESSO Station

Fisher took his foot off the accelerator, braked softly, and turned off the road onto the right shoulder. Then he made a U-turn and started home.

"This clock must be slow," he said with a slight movement of his chin to indicate the clock on the dashboard.

"The clock in the Esso station had the same time," said Bennett.

"What Esso station?"

"The one we passed just before you turned around. See? That one."

The Gazelle

Bennett said, "I've got an erection," and then lapsed into silence.

164

"What's wrong?" said Fisher.

"Nothing."

"How come you look sad? Does the erection make you sad?"

"I get erections nine times a day," said Bennett with a scowl. "What do you want me to do? Have a party every time my prick stands up?"

"Do you really get erections nine times a day?"

"Of course. Don't you?"

"No," said Fisher. "Once or twice. Sometimes I don't get any at all. Sometimes I go for a whole week without one."

"You're kidding."

"No."

"You're lucky. Me, every time I try to make some kind of peace with myself, my thing stands up."

"Why don't you just go out and get laid?"

"Because there's nobody around these days to do it with."

"Then why don't you just go and do it with yourself?"

"I do, Fisher. Lately, five and six times a day. But it doesn't help. It just wears me out and leaves me empty, and then ten minutes later I'm stiff again anyway."

"I'm getting embarrassed," said Fisher.

"Drop it then. I'm sorry I brought it up."

"Is that supposed to be a play on words?"

"No. Just drop it."

"Is that the main point of what you wanted to tell me then? That you get nine erections a day?"

"What are you getting angry about?"

"I'm getting angry about that first you come out with this incredible boast of nine erections a day, and

165

then you get a pitiful look on your face, like you're asking me to be sorry for you!"

"I'm not asking you to be sorry for me."

"Well, that's how it comes across." Fisher's jaw was trembling, and his cheeks were flushed.

"I'm sorry I said anything," said Bennett.

"Don't give me that. Go on and finish. Or was that the whole bit? If it was, you can go to hell. Anybody who is sad because he gets nine erections a day ought to have his head examined!" Suddenly tears came into Fisher's eyes.

Bennett was shocked and bewildered. "What's wrong?" he said.

"Oh, Jesus, Jesus," said Fisher in anguish. "Just give me a cigarette."

Bennett lit a cigarette and passed it. "Here."

"Thanks," Fisher said.

"I can see how it might have sounded like a boast, Fisher, but I just . . . I don't know . . . I just thought that most guys our age were in the same boat . . . I mean, I thought that I was talking about a condition we had in common . . . and, see, if you can believe me that that's what I thought, then me telling you that I get nine erections a day can't really be seen as a boast . . . "

"What about the erection? Have you still got it?"

"Yes."

"Do you want me to pull over, so you can go into the woods and spill it?"

"Take it easy on the sarcasm."

"I wasn't being sarcastic. I really will pull over if you want me to."

166

"I'll ride it out, okay? Just drive. You see, the thing that's bugging me about this erection is . . . the image . . . the image that goes with it. Why are you smiling?"

"Because you get images."

"Why is that funny? Doesn't everyone?"

"I don't. Well, sometimes I get an image . . . but vague . . . like an image of some kind of situation, or . . . never mind . . . "

Bennett stared intently at his friend. "Go ahead," he urged.

"No, no," said Fisher. "Tell me about your image. Wait. I bet I know. You have an image of something you feel guilty about, and you want me to be your confessor."

"No," said Bennett. "First of all, if there's one thing you don't look like, Fisher, it is a confessor."

"What is that supposed to mean?"

"I'm not sure. Just leave it alone."

"What is the second of all?"

"The second of all is that I don't feel guilty about this image. Well, maybe a little."

"What is it then?"

"It's you. Your face. And I wanted to tell you . . . because I probably won't ever see you again, and . . . and . . . what the hell am I saying! Am I allowed to say such a thing? What are you *smiling* about?"

"I don't know. Go ahead."

"Well, it's not like I want to . . . to *have* you or anything . . . or maybe I do . . . I don't know . . . maybe I do! All I know for sure is that your face, it . . . it . . . sometimes in class I'd look at it, specially the mouth, and I'd start to get crazy . . . the eyes, the mouth, the whole shape of the face . . . it's like a woman's face, you know . . ."

"Is it just my face then?"

"Mainly. But, I guess, maybe the arms too, and the shoulders and neck . . . there is something about the way they curve . . . but from the waist down, forget it, your hips are too narrow . . . and, also, just the idea that you have a thing between your legs, I can't deal with that. Jesus! What the hell am I saying! You're blushing. I'm sorry. Christ, what the hell am I saying! Look, you have to promise never to tell anyone I said these things to you. Wait, wait, don't say anything yet. I have to tell you a story.

"One time I went to the zoo. This was just last summer. I went to the Bronx Zoo. And there was a gazelle there. Just an ordinary gazelle. Have you ever seen a gazelle? And this gazelle . . . I don't know if it was male or female . . . but it was lying . . . or, rather, reclining . . . reclining on the ground . . . on its belly, with its head up and looking around at this and that . . . and its rear end was curved up . . . and the knees of its hind legs were bent . . . and the shape of the whole body from the neck down was very much like the shape of a woman reclining on her side with her knees bent and one hip in the air. Can you picture that? That curve? Anyway, I stood there looking at that gazelle . . . it must have been about thirty yards away . . . and I was looking at it through a wrought-iron fence . . . and all of a sudden I got an erection . . . and I thought to myself, 'Do I want to *have* that animal?' And the fact is that I actually had to think about it for a while before I

168

finally decided: who needs it. But the shape of it . . . of that animal, it . . . it . . . "

"It got to you," interrupted Fisher, summing up impatiently.

"Yes."

"So, what you're saying is that I am just like that gazelle for you, just another shape that you happen to get off on."

"Hey, wait. What's going on? Are you offended?"

"You're damn right I'm offended."

"Look, Fisher, this wasn't an easy thing for me to say."

"It sounded pretty easy to me."

"I think you're just ticked off because I said that your hips are narrow."

"Look, what *is* it with you?" said Fisher with contempt and revulsion. "Is that what love and sex are all about for you? Shapes and more shapes? Is that all you're looking for in life? Some *shape?*"

"I don't know, I don't know!" cried Bennett in despair. "I was just trying to be honest with you and tell you about something that is important to me and drives me wild, and that you . . . that *you*, Fisher, are at this moment very intimately *connected* with. Christ! Why are you so angry!"

"Because it's not *me* that is connected with you! It's just some kind of a *shape!*"

"I don't believe this conversation."

"What? Stop muttering."

"I said, I don't believe this conversation!"

"Neither do I," said Fisher. "You're sick."

169

"Dammit, I'm sorry I ever started this. Why am I sick? Because of the gazelle? Is that it? If that's it, then you didn't understand me at all."

"Maybe 'sick' is the wrong word. You're just naive, that's all. Naive."

"How am I naive?"

"For one thing, up until a minute ago you thought that everybody in the world gets nine erections a day."

"I never said that. What I was talking about was guys like you and me . . . like, guys our age . . . "

"Well? That's naive!"

"Okay, okay!"

"And then, when you were talking about the gazelle, I had the feeling that you thought that this was some kind of very grand, universal-type experience, and that you were expecting me to say, 'I know precisely what you mean, my good fellow, because I had a similar experience once, only it was with a giraffe!' And that then you and I would have, like, this very agreeable, terribly enlightened 'communication' thing going between us."

"You're wrong. I wasn't expecting that at all."

"Then why did you tell me about it?"

"Let's drop it."

"No. Come on. Tell me."

"It's just a problem that is bothering me, and I wanted to talk about it."

"I don't understand. What's the problem?"

"Mainly what it is, is that I can't figure out if the erection I get when I look at your face really has anything to do with you."

"Oh, great . . . great!" exclaimed Fisher, and he rolled his eyes up, as if to invoke the compassion of someone on the roof of the car.

"Jesus, Fisher, everything I say in*sults* you," said Bennett with irritation.

"That's right. All of it insults me. What did you expect?"

"I don't know. I guess you were right before. I guess I did expect you to understand and say that you had some sort of similar experience . . . not with a gazelle maybe . . . but . . . I don't know. Look, I know it couldn't be exactly the same for you because women don't really turn you on, right?"

"I hate that expression. 'Turn you on.' What does it mean? It sounds like you're talking about a water spigot."

"Okay! I won't use it then. Let's put it this way: Women don't excite you sexually. How's that?"

"It sounds like a textbook."

"Whatever it sounds like, it's true, isn't it? Your thing doesn't stand up for a feminine shape. How's that?"

"It stinks."

"Well, it's the best I can do! Do you want to sit here and talk about words all night? Listen, just let me finish what I am trying to say. Okay? Look, I guess I did expect . . . that . . . that you would understand, because, after all, you say you're in love, right? So, *some*thing attracts you, right? So, if it's not a feminine shape, then, okay, it's a masculine shape. Right? That's logical, isn't it? So then, maybe you might go to the zoo one day and see, like, say, a

171

gorilla. A gorilla is masculine, right? And say that you're horny that day, okay? And you look at this gorilla, and . . . presto! Your thing stands up. See? In response to the shape."

"A gorilla? Man, you are out of your mind. You don't understand anything at all. It's not shapes that excite me."

"It's not?" Bennett was amazed.

"No! I told you that before. You just don't listen. Have you still got the erection?"

"Not really."

"What does that mean?"

"It means, I have half of it."

"Half an erection?"

"Yes," said Bennett uneasily.

Suddenly Fisher moved his foot from the accelerator to the brake and swerved over to the shoulder of the road and stopped the car and turned off the lights and the motor.

"What are you doing?" said Bennett in alarm.

"Let me touch it," said Fisher. "Maybe I can bring it back to its full size."

"Hey, wait . . . " Bennett drew away and gripped the handle of the door.

"Are you scared?" said Fisher. "Are you going to leave the car?"

"Just cool it," said Bennett.

"It's a long walk home."

"Come on, Fisher. You're giving me the creeps."

"Why? I won't attack you or anything. In fact, I won't do anything that you don't want me to do. I just asked, that's all. You seem to want to know what

172

gets me. Well, that's it. An erection. That gets me. And I don't even have to see it. In fact, *not* seeing it, and yet knowing it's there, is even stronger. Just the knowing. Can you understand that?"

"It sounds kinky."

"Maybe. But it's not. I'm not talking about veils and disguises like a freak in a perverted house of assignation in some whacked-out French movie like the one that Steinmetz showed at his party last year. For those characters I guess it really is the veil or the disguise that gets them. But I couldn't care less about that kind of a circus. I don't even understand it. What I'm telling you is that it is the erection itself that gets me. Not that the shape puts me off. Sometimes I can see a penis, or a picture of one, and if the shape is handsome, it might stir me up. But it's not the shape, ultimately, that I am after. There is something else that I want. Something deeper. But you, David, you want the shape, and only the shape, which to me is superficial, and in any case illusory. And that's probably why you're so insensitive. You didn't even understand before that you were teasing me in some really cruel way with your boast about nine erections. Did you understand that? Did you?"

"No. I swear I didn't, Fisher, and I'm sorry."

"Don't swear. Look, there are people in the world, people like me, who are lusting after something that has no shape. That's all I want to tell you, okay?"

"No, it's not okay," said Bennett grimly.

"Why not?"

"Because you're stacking the deck, dammit. You're trying to prove that you're superior to me, and I . . .

I don't buy it. In fact, it's a lot of crap. I have high-class longings, too!"

"Are you talking about intellectual passions?"

"What's wrong with intellectual passions?"

"Nothing. I have them, too. But they don't get my prick up. And they don't get yours up either."

"How do you know?"

"Do they?"

"No. They don't. But, so what!"

"So nothing. It's just altogether beside the point, that's all."

"Hold it, Fisher . . . just hold it one . . . minute!" said Bennett, confused and angry, and extremely nervous, as if he were being threatened by a siege of hostile forces which he might hold at bay and conquer, only if he could find, somehow, the right words. "What you're trying to prove to me . . . " he went on after a moment, "what you're trying to prove is that queers are superior to . . . to non-queers, right?"

Fisher laughed. "No," he said. "Queerness has nothing to do with this. In fact, there are a lot of queers who don't feel like I do at all. Take Andy. He's like you. He's into shapes."

"Who's Andy?"

"Andy is the queer I am going to live with. I've had the same argument with him a dozen times."

"Look, Fisher, I'm sorry I used that word."

"Forget it. I don't mind. In fact, at the moment I even like it."

"What kind of shapes is this Andy into? Masculine shapes?"

"What is a masculine shape?"

174

"Well . . . "

"The masculine shape," said Fisher, "is a straight line, and there are no straight lines in nature."

"You have this all figured out, I see," said Bennett spitefully.

"Like I said, I've had this argument before. In my book, the whole visible universe is curves, nothing but curves, a very exclusive, feminine circus. And all that guys like you want to do, actually, is fuck it."

"Maybe. Okay? Maybe! But . . . tell me more about this Andy. You say he's into shapes. And therefore, according to you, he's into the feminine, right?"

Fisher looked at Bennett seductively from under lowered lids and licked his upper lip. "He is into *me*."

"Jesus Christ, Fisher, don't look at me like that."

Fisher smiled. "Why not?"

"Start the motor," said Bennett.

"In a minute," said Fisher. He took the key out of the ignition and touched Bennett's knee gently and added, "I'll be right back."

"Where are you going?"

"I'm thirsty. There's a thermos of coffee in the trunk. I'll be right back."

Fisher opened the door and stepped out of the car.

"Why did you take the keys?" said Bennett. "Are you afraid I'll drive off and leave you here?"

Fisher shut the door and then ducked his head and rested his forearms on the bottom of the window.

"Maybe I am afraid of that," he said. "But the main reason I took the keys is . . . that I need them to open the trunk."

He smiled and then went around to the back of the car.

He stayed back there far too long just to get a thermos, though, and eventually Bennett lost patience. He turned around to look through the rear window, but the lid of the trunk blocked his view, so he rolled down the window in the door and stuck his head out.

"What the hell is taking so long?" he said.

"Nothing, nothing," answered Fisher, and there was an anxious tremor in his voice. "Be right there. I have five suitcases back here, and I can't remember which one I put the thermos in."

"I'll come out and help you look."

"No, no, wait! Here it is! Okay, I got it. I'll be right there. I just have to close up the suitcases."

A minute later the lid of the trunk slammed shut.

Bennett turned to look through the rear window again, and this time he saw Fisher.

"Oh, Christ," muttered Bennett. "What the hell did he do to himself?"

Fisher was lit by the moon and also by a bluish light from a highway lamp on the opposite side of the road. He appeared to have done something to his face. His eyelashes appeared to be darker and longer and his lips fuller and luminous.

But of course, thought Bennett, all this may be just a trick of the moon or the theatrical highway lamp. He turned away and faced the windshield and folded his arms across his chest. Soon he heard footsteps on the gravel. They were crisp and light, yet slow. Fisher ordinarily had a rapid stride.

"Want a sip?"

On turning to the voice, Bennett discovered Fisher leaning in the window of the rear door and offering the thermos.

176

Bennett took the thermos. "Thanks," he said.

Fisher opened the door and got into the back seat. He was wearing only his shirt now, and his legs were bare. On his feet were silver shoes. Each shoe was fashioned out of a few narrow straps that criss-crossed prettily, a thin sole, and a tapered spike that served as the heel. His legs had no hair on them. They were smooth and pale and remarkably like a young girl's. Over the shirt he wore a belt drawn closely around the waist, so that the hips were revealed, in fact, as round and plump.

He lay on his side across the back seat, propping himself on one elbow, his hip almost as high as his shoulder, his legs flexed at the knees.

"Is this how the gazelle was?" he said.

Bennett gaped in astonishment, then turned away. He placed the thermos on top of the dashboard.

"Why are you turning away from me?" said Fisher.

"Dammit, this is so *weird!*" said Bennett, staring at the windshield.

"Turn around and look at me," said Fisher gently.

"No . . . Jesus, it's so weird! What the hell are you doing? Please, Fisher, go and get dressed again. I don't know how to deal with this . . . really . . . Jesus . . . Jesus, Jesus . . . "

"Just look at me."

"No! I'm not . . . I absolutely will not look at you. Do you hear me? So go back to the trunk and get dressed. We're going home. Do you hear me? Christ!"

"I want you to look at me. Just once."

"No, Fisher. Why should I? What did you do to yourself? Is that make-up on your face?"

177

"Not really. Just a little, very light pastel rouge on the lips, and something that makes the eyelashes seem longer. Do you like it?"

"Look, *please* . . . let's go."

"Why? Are you afraid?"

"Yes. I'm afraid."

"What are you afraid of?"

"I don't know!" cried Bennett in anguish, and then, startled by the emotion in his own voice, he glanced quickly at the rearview mirror and met Fisher's eyes.

"You're looking," said Fisher, smiling in the mirror.

Bennett looked away at once and slapped the dashboard excitedly.

"Dammit, I get it now!" he cried, as if something extraordinary had just been revealed to him, and then he began to talk to himself under his breath in trivial exclamations.

"What are you saying?" said Fisher.

"Nothing."

"What is it that you get?"

"I'll tell you in a minute," said Bennett. "First answer a question for me, all right? Did you . . . did you ever have any kind of sex with Leskov?"

There was silence for a few moments.

Then Bennett turned around. "Did you?" he persisted, looking directly at Fisher.

"Yes. I did."

"When?"

"Two weeks ago was the first time."

"What happened?"

"I don't want to talk about it."

"Where did it happen? In a car?"

"I don't want to talk about it!" cried Fisher with ferocity, and he swung his legs around and sat up, his eyes gleaming with anger and hatred.

"You mean, he *had* you? Leskov *had* you?"

Fisher smiled knowingly. The anger and hatred vanished from his eyes.

"You're jealous, aren't you," he said.

"Jealous! Are you crazy? Why should I be jealous? And who is it do you suppose I'm jealous of?"

"Both of us," said Fisher with quiet confidence. "You are jealous of me, because I had Leskov. And you are jealous of Leskov, because he had me."

"What? Man, you are really . . . really conceited! Do you know that? What an egotist you are! I swear, I never heard anything like that in my whole life! Do you really think you're so desireable? I mean, do you? Jesus!" Bennett turned all the way around and, kneeling on the seat, began to gesture emphatically with both hands. "A minute ago I said I get it, and you said get what, and I didn't answer, because . . . because I wasn't really sure. But now I'm sure. Oh, brother, am I sure! You think that I am shallow and insensitive because I'm into shapes, right?"

"Not because you are into them, but because you lust after them."

"All right! Lust! I lust after shapes! And you don't! I see that now. You really don't! You just want to *be* the shapes. You want to *be* the shapes that guys like me go crazy for. Isn't that right, Fisher? Isn't it? Isn't it? Answer!"

"Why don't you come into the back seat for a minute?" said Fisher in a soothing, maternal voice. "You look like you want to cry."

"What! Are you crazy?"

"Come back here, and let me hold you."

"Stop talking to me like that, Fisher. Jesus, it's so . . . so weird!"

"What are you afraid of?"

"I'm not afraid of anything!" cried Bennett, and he lunged forward and seized Fisher by the shoulders. "Do you hear me? So shut up! Shut up!"

"Not so rough. . ." said Fisher, and suddenly his eyes filled with tears, and a tremor went through him; then he laid the back of his head on the top of the seat and stared up at the roof with his lips parted and his breathing uncommonly deep.

"Fisher, Fisher, what's wrong with you!" cried Bennett in alarm, and he clambered over the seat into the back and took Fisher's face in both hands. "Are you all right? Fisher, speak to me. Are you all right?"

Fisher closed his eyes. "Just touch me," he said.

At once Bennett let go of Fisher's face and looked at it for a moment. Then he touched it again, but this time tentatively, and just with one hand, caressing the cheekbone with his thumb. Then he sat down, took out a cigarette, tapped it three times on his knuckles, and returned it to the pack. Then he undid the laces on his sneakers and took them off. Then he took off his cotton socks, his trousers, his waterproof jacket and his shirt. All this took some time. It was a clumsy exercise in such a confined space, and, moreover, he contemplated each article for a while after he had removed it. When he was naked, he got up on his knees on the seat, shivering a little in the cold air. Ordinarily in cold air his penis got small and retreated, but now it was erect. He took it in his hand and began to move the tip lightly across Fisher's pale skin, scanning the soft curves of the limbs, the waist, and hips, and even the mouth and the rims of the eyes. Then like the leader in a dance he put one hand in the small of Fisher's back and one on his shoulder and got him to turn and kneel on the seat and went into him with some effort, eliciting from him a painful ambiguous protest, which subsided shortly, as the two men began to rock back and forth and Fisher began to speak. He spoke in a rush. The terms in which he spoke were familiar, but the voice was not the Fisher that Bennett knew. In fact, the voice was altogether alien, specially at the conclusion, when Fisher began to howl like a madman. Therefore Bennett, even in the depths of his own pleasure, was baffled and disquieted and silent.

At the end Fisher laughed briefly and lowered his chest to the seat and cradled his head in the crook of his arm. And Bennett also lay down, nestling the side of his face between Fisher's shoulder blades.

For a while the two friends lay quite peacefully.

Then Bennett sat up and got his clothes and put them on.

"If you don't mind me driving your car," he said when he was dressed, "I'm going to take myself home now."

By way of an answer Fisher sat up and gave Bennett the key ring.

Then the two friends climbed over into the front seat, and Bennett started the motor. Though already erect again, he pressed the accelerator resolutely and, turning on the lights, guided the Plymouth onto the road.

TRUE PROFESSIONS

As the Plymouth pulled up to the curb in front of Bennett's apartment, Fisher said that he would like to come in for a few minutes to wash up and change into more presentable clothes before getting back on the road. The two friends had been silent for nearly half an hour, ever since Bennett took the wheel, so that Fisher's rather ordinary request, spoken in a subdued hoarse voice, projected itself into the already charged atmosphere with a disturbing force, and Bennett, disarmed, consented uneasily; he shut off the motor and the lights, then slipped out of his jacket and handed it to his friend, telling him to tie the sleeves around his waist, just as a precaution, because, as Fisher would have to go to the trunk to get fresh clothes, the opening and closing of the lid was bound to alert all the neighborhood insomniacs. Bennett also suggested that Fisher remove the high-heeled shoes, which were likely to arouse at least as much interest as the bare legs and besides would make an awful racket.

"Why don't I just leave the shoes on and forget the jacket," said Fisher, "and go out as I am, and just sway my hips a little, and then if anybody sees me, there will be no problem, because they'll just take me for a woman."

"Forget it," said Bennett.

"But I could pass," protested Fisher.

"I said forget it."

"But the ground is like ice! I'll freeze my feet off out there!"

"What size shoe do you wear?"

"Nine."

At once Bennett pulled his sneakers off. "Try these," he said, handing them to Fisher. "They're ten and a half. They'll be a little big, but they'll do the job."

"But what about you?"

"I've got thick socks, and I can make it to the door in half a second. But you have to go and open the trunk and carry your stuff. It will take you a minute or two. Put the sneakers on."

Bennett reached into his trouser pocket to get the keys to the door of his apartment, but then, remembering that he had deliberately left the door unlocked, he withdrew his hand and got out of the car and ran up the walk, the soles of his feet stinging with the cold.

With one turn of the knob, he opened the apartment door and hurried inside; then he went to the front window and, after drawing the curtains shut, parted them a little with one hand, so that he could peer out at the street.

A minute or two passed before Fisher got out of the car. He slammed the door and scraped the over-sized sneakers on the rough cement of the road noisily as he walked back to the trunk. He had to fiddle with the lock and pound his fist three times on the lid to get it open. Then he shuffled a few suitcases around, knocking them together again and again before he got the one he wanted. This one he pulled out and let drop on the ground, after which he put both hands on top of the lid of the trunk, slamming it violently four times before it caught in the latch.

At last he picked up the suitcase, a rather large heavy one that caused him to tilt to one side to maintain his balance as he walked. He walked up the path quickly and awkwardly, a clownish eccentric fugitive in his oversized footwear, his bare legs, the jacket tied around his waist.

The moment Fisher got to the doorstep, Bennett hurried over to open the door. He took Fisher by the arm, ushering him inside, shut the door noiselessly, locked it, and slipped the chain in the latch.

Fisher set the suitcase down in the middle of the room, kicked off the sneakers and flung the jacket onto the sofa. He was breathing heavily. His nose was red from the cold. He rubbed his hands together and shivered and hunched up his shoulders and puckered and vibrated his lips to make a sound like a child

185

imitating an airplane or automobile engine. He crossed his arms over his chest and rubbed his shoulders and danced back and forth from one bare foot to the other.

"Would you like some coffee?" said Bennett. "Or a can of soup?"

"No, no," said Fisher. "Just hold me for a minute."

"You have to get dressed, Fisher, and leave. You have a long trip ahead of you."

"I don't want to go anymore. I want to stay here. With you. I love you."

"You're getting confused, Fisher. It's not me you love. It's a guy in New Hampshire. Remember? You promised him."

Tears came to Fisher's eyes. After a moment he said, "I can't leave."

"What do you mean you can't leave? You have to leave."

"Don't you want me?"

Bennett went and picked up his jacket from the sofa. "Here," he said, "come sit down on the sofa for a minute."

Fisher came over and took Bennett's hand and sat down.

Gently Bennett drew his hand away and walked across the room and sat in a straight-backed chair, draping the jacket across his lap and leaning forward with his elbows on his knees.

The phone rang.

Bennett was startled. He glanced at Fisher, whose eyes suddenly livened up with anxiety.

"If it's Olive, I'm not here," Fisher said in a low confidential tone.

"I hate lying," said Bennett.

"Please," pleaded Fisher.

"I don't like being in the middle of this," said Bennett, going to the phone.

"If you tell her I'm not here, you won't be in the middle of anything."

"That's one way to look at it." Bennett put his hand on top of the phone and glanced at the clock over the refrigerator. The time was about ten minutes after four.

"You'd better answer," said Fisher.

"What for? I'm not up to it, Fisher."

"If you don't answer, Olive will be ringing the doorbell in another ten minutes, I guarantee it."

"What is she, a witch?"

"She's just very connected. Not with everybody. Just with me."

"It must be creepy to be married to someone like that, who knows where you are all the time. No wonder you left her."

"I used to like it."

"Really? Why, for godsakes?"

"I just did. Anyway that wasn't the problem."

"Maybe it wasn't," said Bennett, "but it ought to have been."

Abruptly Bennett tore the receiver from its cradle and delivered a stern challenging "hello" into the mouthpiece.

The voice on the other end of the line was a woman's but it was not Olive; it was Sarah.

"David? Is that you?" she said, clearly surprised and put off by the stern angry voice that had greeted her.

187

"Sarah?" said Bennett, with special emphasis for the benefit of Fisher, who wrinkled his brow inquisitively and exchanged with his friend a puzzled, amused glance.

"I've been trying to reach you for hours!" said Sarah.

"I just got in a few minutes ago."

"Where have you been!"

"At the party. It ran late. And I stayed to clean up."

"But I called you at the party two hours ago! They said it broke up early, and that you'd left."

"I went out for a bit to get cigarettes and then I came back. They must have thought I'd left for good. Also my bike was stolen, and I had to walk home, and it took me a long time. What's up?"

"Dimitri is gone, David. He had wanted to talk to you. He said it was important. He made me call everybody. I even called your parents about an hour ago."

"My parents?"

"Dimitri said that he saw them at the play, and that maybe you went back to Long Island with them."

"My parents weren't at the play."

"Of course they were. I just spoke to them, and they went on and on about it! David, why are you lying?"

"I'm not lying. What I meant was that I . . . I never introduced them to Dimitri . . . or anybody . . . so there was no way for him to know that they were there . . . do you see?"

"He said that he saw them with you backstage after the play, and that you look just like your mother."

"What did you tell them?"

"I just said that I was trying to find you. I suppose I worried them a bit. I promised them I'd have you call as soon as I found you. You should call right away, David."

"At this hour?"

"What's the difference!"

"The difference is that they like their sleep. To them sleep is sacred. Like a god."

"Goddess."

"What?"

"Goddess," said Sarah. "Sleep is a goddess."

"How did you get their number?"

"I called information in Nassau County."

"How did you know my father's first name?"

"Dimitri knew it."

"He did?"

"Yes."

"But there are three John Bennetts in Nassau County. I once looked it up."

"I got all three numbers."

"You mean you woke up all three John Bennetts in Nassau County?"

"Only two. I got your father on the second try . . . Oh, God, they're here! There's somebody at the door. I've got to put the phone down a minute. But don't hang up. Do you hear? I'll be right back. Don't hang up!"

Bennett winced at a sharp clattering noise at the other end of the line, as if the receiver had been put on a table and then slipped off onto the floor. In the background he could make out the sound of a door opening and muffled voices.

"What's going on?" said Fisher.

"Leskov is up to something again," said Bennett. "He's going to drive that woman crazy."

"What is she saying?"

"She says he's been looking for me tonight."

Sarah came back on the line again. "David? Are you still there?"

"Yes," said Bennett, "I'm here."

"Don't hang up. I'll be right back. Don't hang up!"

There was another clattering noise, but less harsh. Apparently this time Sarah had managed to put the phone down without it falling off the table. In the background, once more, was the sound of a door opening; not the front door though; Leskov's front door had a terrible creak in the hinges; the door that just opened was relatively quiet.

Bennett said, "She's gone again."

"What the hell is going on there?" said Fisher.

"Some people have just turned up. It sounds lik a party."

"Is Leskov there?"

"No. She said he went off somewhere. But I knew he wasn't there as soon as I heard her voice, because whenever he's around, she speaks very carefully, and at the moment she sounds like she doesn't give a damn what she says. She's not even being polite. She even snapped at me once."

"About what?"

"Sleep. When I said that to my parents sleep was sacred like a god, suddenly she got this very critical irritated tone and said that sleep was not a god, but a goddess."

190

"She picked that up from Leskov," said Fisher. "A couple of weeks ago I heard Leskov give her a whole lecture about how sleep was a goddess."

"Why did he do that?"

Sarah came on the line again.

"I'm back," she said almost in a whisper, apparently to keep her voice from her guests.

"What's going on, Sarah?" said Bennett. "What did Dimitri want to talk to me about?"

"I don't know exactly. But it was very, very important to him. He got really crazy about it. Out of control. I've never seen him like that."

"Where is he now, Sarah?"

"He's gone . . . gone . . . don't you understand?"

"How long ago was it that he left? Is it possible that he is on his way over here? To my place?"

"Candles? I'm not sure. Maybe I have some in the kitchen. In the sink over the cupboard . . . I mean the cupboard over the sink! Wait. I'll get them for you . . . "

"What's this about candles? What the hell are you talking about?"

"I'm not talking to you, David. I've got to put the phone down for a minute. Don't go away!"

Bennett heard the receiver on the other end of the line clatter on the table again; then there were muffled voices and footsteps. He heard cupboard doors opening and shutting noisily in the kitchen, and also the clinking of plates and glasses.

Bennett said, "Get dressed, Fisher. I think Leskov may be on his way over here."

"Jesus Christ," said Fisher, leaping to his feet, and he hurried over to his suitcase and knelt in front of it. "What the hell is going on?" he added, snapping the latches open.

"Drag your suitcase over here and hold onto the phone for me for a minute. I want to go and have a look out the window."

Hurriedly Fisher walked sideways on his knees, dragging the suitcase with him, until he got close enough to reach the phone. Then he took the receiver and propped it between his chin and shoulder and started to rummage around in the suitcase for clothes.

Bennett went to the window and, pushing aside the curtain, looked up and down the street.

"Is he out there?" said Fisher.

"Not yet."

"Is the door locked?"

"Yes, I . . . Jesus, the door!"

"What about it?"

"I left it unlocked all night tonight!"

"What did you do that for?"

"I don't know."

"Do you have anything valuable here?"

"Not really. My typewriter . . . that's about all."

"Is it still here?"

"I haven't looked. It's in the bedroom. But that's not what I'm worried about."

"What are you worried about?"

"Leskov! If the door was unlocked, Leskov could have walked right in! You see?"

"So what? Do you think he would steal your goddamn typewriter or something?"

"That's not the point. The point is that he could still be here."

Fisher looked up from the suitcase. "Where?" he said suspiciously.

"In the apartment."

"Are you out of your mind?"

"I'm just saying it's a possibility."

"Is his car out front?"

"No, but . . . "

"So if his car is not out front, where is it?"

"Maybe he parked it around the corner," said Bennett. "Or maybe he took a cab. He's always taking cabs. Sometimes he doesn't feel like driving, and he takes a cab. And it always costs him a fortune because he tips like King Farouk."

"You're not serious, are you?"

"About him being in the apartment? Yes, I'm serious. I have a . . . a . . . " Here Bennett lowered his voice: "I have this feeling . . . like a . . . a . . . "

"Jesus, you're shaking," said Fisher, alarmed.

Bennett crossed the room and stopped just before the threshhold to the bedroom. "Leskov," he called out in a strong, stern voice, "Are you in there?"

"Jesus," muttered Fisher, and he scrambled to his feet in a panic and hurriedly got into a pair of blue denim trousers, all the while keeping the phone propped under his chin.

"I'm coming in," announced Bennett, and he walked into the bedroom.

"Is the typewriter there?" said Fisher, fumbling with the trouser buttons.

"Yes, the typewriter is here." Bennett went to the bedroom closet and flung open the door. Finding nobody inside, he hurried to the bathroom and found nobody there either.

"Oh . . . hi, Sarah," said Fisher in a raised voice for the benefit of Bennett. "No, no, it's Jimmy. What? No, no, David's in the . . . the bathroom . . . he'll be right out . . . What? . . . Me? . . . Oh, I just got here a couple of minutes ago. I had some books that I'd borrowed from David last week, and I stopped by to return them, because I knew he needed them for the paper he is writing for nineteenth-century lit . . . What? . . . No, no, I had a few other loose ends to tie up before I left. Wait. Here's David."

Rushing back into the livingroom Bennett grabbed the receiver and clapped his hand over the mouthpiece. "Why the hell did you let her know you were here?" he said in a fierce whisper.

"She was on the line . . . she . . . she was talking . . . what was I supposed to do?"

"You should have signaled me!"

"How? You were in the other room! I couldn't even see you!"

"Lower your voice."

"I couldn't see you," repeated Fisher in a softer whisper.

"You should have put the phone down and come and got me."

"I thought you wanted me to answer . . . "

"Never mind! What did you tell her?"

"Didn't you hear me?"

"Yes, yes, I heard."

"So why did you ask me what I told her, for godsakes!"

"Never mind!" said Bennett; then he thrust the receiver back into Fisher's hand. "Just hold this again for a minute. I'll be right back. And . . . and don't talk to her anymore, for godsakes . . . Not one more word, do you hear?"

With this Bennett rushed over to the closet at the far end of the livingroom and, opening the door, muttered angrily under his breath.

Fisher clapped his hand over the mouthpiece of the phone. "You didn't seriously expect to find him in the closet, did you?" he said.

Bennett shut the closet door. "He's in this apartment somewhere, I tell you."

"Don't be ridiculous," said Fisher. "You looked everywhere!"

"I tell you, he's here. I can feel it!"

"You're shaking . . . "

"Leskov is in the apartment, Fisher. Do you hear what I am saying to you? I can feel it just as plain as if his breath were blowing on the back of my neck—"

"Slow down . . . really . . . slow down . . . you're scaring me . . . "

"Give me the phone," said Bennett, and he took the receiver angrily out of Fisher's hand; then he lowered his chin and spoke into the mouthpiece. "Sarah?" he said gently.

"Jimmy?" said Sarah.

"No, it's me again," said Bennett.

"David?"

"Yes. Listen to me, Sarah. You have got to tell me where Dimitri is."

"I . . . I . . . I told you . . . He's gone . . . he . . . he . . . "

195

"I know he's gone. I know you told me that. But didn't he at least give you some hint about where he was going? Did he say maybe that he was on his way to my place? . . . Sarah? . . . Are you there?"

Bennett heard the sound of Sarah sniffling and blowing her nose.

"You're not understanding me, David," she said with reproach in a hoarse, tearful voice. "Dimitri is not gone gone. He is gone dead."

Bennett stared at the tabletop on which the telephone sat.

"What's going on?" said Fisher. "You look like you're going to pass out."

"Quiet, Fisher." said Bennett.

"What?" said Sarah. "Did you say something?"

Bennett raised his voice. "I was talking to Fisher."

"David, I need you to come over here. Right away. I've called Dimitri's parents, but they won't be able to get here for another ten hours. I also called my own parents, but they're in Florida at the moment, and they won't be able to get here maybe until tomorrow morning. Alice is on her way over to help with Annie when she wakes up. Otherwise there really isn't anybody in town I want to deal with right now—not for a few hours anyway—except you—I need your help right now, David. Just get a cab, and I'll pay for it. Don't have Jimmy bring you—unless he can just drop you off . . . Don't tell him I said that. Maybe later in the day he can come over, if he likes . . . but not right this minute . . . I couldn't deal with Jimmy right this minute . . . David? . . . Are you there?"

"Yes, yes . . . I'm here . . . "

"Can you come?"

"Yes . . . I'll be right there . . . "

"It's just that . . . " Here Sarah spoke in an emphatic whisper: ". . . that I have this house full of strangers at the moment . . . and . . . and I don't like being alone with them . . . "

"What strangers? Sarah? Are they listening to you?"

"Yes . . . "

"What the hell is going on?" said Fisher.

Bennett signaled angrily at Fisher to keep quiet.

"Just tell me this one thing," persisted Fisher, lowering his voice. "Does she know where he is?"

Bennett clamped his hand over the mouthpiece. "I warn you," he said. "Don't interrupt again."

Indignantly Fisher pulled a pair of tennis sneakers and a pair of thick white socks out of the suitcase and went to the front window. He peered out into the street, then went and dragged a chair close to the window and set about putting on the socks and sneakers, all the while watching the street anxiously.

When Bennett put his ear back to the receiver, he heard Sarah asking him a question: "Do you have one?"

"One what?" said Bennett.

"David . . . have you been listening to me?"

"Yes, yes . . . every word . . . it's just that Fisher was just talking to me . . . and . . . I couldn't hear you for a minute . . . "

"Did you hear what I was saying about a suit and tie?"

"No . . . "

"Do you have a suit and tie?"

"Of course."

"You'll have to wear it."

"When?"

"Now. When you come here. You are coming, aren't you?"

"Yes, yes."

"Is it a dark suit?"

"It's gray flannel."

"Is it a dark gray?"

"Medium."

"That will have to do then. It's just that I don't want you to feel uncomfortable. All the men here are wearing black—black suits—"

"Black?"

"There's a cab pulling up to the curb down the street," said Fisher excitedly.

Bennett waved a hand in exasperation.

"The cab is just sitting there. I think there is a passenger in the back seat," continued Fisher.

Again Bennett waved his hand, and also stamped his foot.

"Listen to me, Sarah," he said. "Did he say anything to you about me?"

"A lot."

"What did he say?"

"That he wanted to see you . . . that . . . that he had to see you . . . that he . . . he had something to tell you . . . "

"Did he say what it was?"

"In a sense . . . but not precisely . . . "

"What do you mean by 'not precisely?' "

"I mean that I have a good idea of what it was."

"Did it have to do with anything that happened the other night? When he and I went to the bars?"

"In a way . . . yes . . . "

"The cab is still sitting there," said Fisher. "The headlights are on, and there is definitely a passenger in the back seat. I can see him moving around . . . "

"Is that Jimmy talking?" said Sarah.

"Yes."

"What's he saying?"

"Nothing. Never mind. Listen, Sarah, where is he now?"

"Who?"

"Dimitri."

"His body is in the bedroom."

"You're sure?"

"What kind of a question is that!"

"It's just a question. You haven't actually told me how any of this happened."

"He was here . . . I was with him . . . he was in bed . . . he died just a little over an hour ago . . . "

"And you're sure? That it's really over?"

"Are you out of your mind? His hands and feet and face are purple. His whole body is like ice. He has no heartbeat and no breath! The doctor was here and wrote out the death certificate!"

"It's just that a few months ago he told me he once studied with one of those yogis who know how to slow down their heartbeat and make themselves look like dead men, and he said that he'd got this trick down pretty good, and that he even once fooled some guy in Morocco just for laughs, and so I thought that maybe . . . you know . . . that . . . "

199

Bennett was interrupted by the sound of Sarah laughing.

"What's so funny?" said Bennett.

"You!" said Sarah in a sparkling voice. "About a half hour before he died, Dimitri predicted that you were going to say something about this yogi trick, and that at first you weren't going to believe that he was really dead . . . that you'd be . . . suspicious . . . you know? . . . I told him I thought he was misjudging you . . . we even had a funny little argument over it near the end . . . "

After a pause, Bennett said, "How did the doctor get there so fast?"

"What's wrong with you, David? You sound like a detective in a B-movie!"

"I don't. I don't sound like a detective at all. Just tell me. How did the doctor get there so fast?"

"He lives across the street," said Sarah with irritation. "Doctor Peterson. He was here a quarter of an hour before the end. He wanted to get Dimitri to the hospital, but Dimitri refused, and I wouldn't give permission because Dimitri hated hospitals. There! Does that satisfy you?"

"Is the doctor still there?"

"For godsakes, David, are you coming over or not? Can't we finish this conversation in person?"

"Yes . . . yes . . . I'm sorry . . . I'm on my way."

"Good. Just don't forget the suit—all right?"

"Right."

"Are you going to have Jimmy drive you?"

"Probably."

"That's all right then. But do not . . . absolutely do not bring him to the door. If you do, I will never forgive you!"

With that Sarah hung up the phone.

Bennett hung up too, then crossed the room and stood quietly behind Fisher, who sat gazing intently out the window at the taxicab parked by the curb about thirty yards down the street. The cab had its headlights on. Clouds of steam poured out of the exhaust pipe. There was a passenger in the back seat. Both the passenger and the driver could be seen in silhouette through the windshield. The passenger appeared to be wearing a wide-brimmed stetson hat and an overcoat with the collar turned up.

"They're still there," said Fisher, his gaze fixed with fascination on the cab.

"Yes, I see," said Bennett, placing one hand affectionately on Fisher's shoulder.

"What do you make of it?"

"That cab comes here every morning on weekdays and picks up a guy with a briefcase, a big fat guy, and takes him to the train station. The fat guy always keeps the cab waiting five or ten minutes. He's a commuter. An accountant, I think, or a lawyer. Works on Wall Street. I don't know who the other passenger is though. Usually the cab is empty when it turns up. Can you make out his face?"

"Just the hat. Leskov has a hat like that."

"Yes, I know. I've seen it."

"Do you think it could be him?"

"I . . . I . . . I don't know . . . "

Fisher stood up quickly and went to his suitcase and pulled out a dark Navy pea-coat and put it on. "Let's go have a look," he said.

"No . . . wait—"

"What's wrong? Are you afraid?"

"Maybe . . . I don't know . . . I . . . I . . . "

"What's going on? What the hell was all that about with Sarah on the telephone?"

"She says that he is dead."

"Leskov is dead?"

"That's what she says."

"What do you mean by 'That's what she says.' Don't you believe her? . . . Speak to me, dammit!"

"I . . . I don't know . . . "

"You mean you think Sarah would lie about a thing like that? Jesus! Are you crazy? Why would she lie!"

"She's married to Leskov, isn't she?"

"So?"

"So Leskov lies."

Fisher stared at Bennett in amazement, started to say something, then checked himself and looked down at his jacket and hurriedly began to do up the buttons.

"What are you doing?" said Bennett.

"I'm going out to have a look at who is in the back of that cab."

"Don't," said Bennett.

"Why not?"

"You'll attract attention. People will talk."

"About what?"

"About whatever people talk about."

"Forget it. I can't stand this one more minute. I'm going." Fisher went to the door decisively and opened it, and a moment later he was hurrying down the sidewalk to the cab.

Bennett parted the curtains slightly with one hand and watched through the window.

Fisher leaned over the hood of the cab to peer at the windshield. Then he went to the rear door and opened it and ducked his head to look into the back seat. At the same time the fat man with the briefcase came out of his house and walked over to the cab, almost colliding with Fisher, who was just about to shut the door and retreat. The fat man stood still for a few moments in an attitude of astonishment and indignation as Fisher ran off down the sidewalk back to Bennett's apartment.

The moment Fisher came through the front door, the fat man shrugged his shoulders and got in the back seat of the cab. He pulled the door shut and the cab drove off. Bennett let go of the curtains and moved away from the window.

Fisher was rubbing his hands together to get them warm.

"It wasn't Leskov," he said.

"You're sure . . .?"

"Sure I'm sure!"

"Maybe he was disguised. You can do incredible stuff with make-up . . . "

Fisher laughed. "Are you serious? Listen . . . this guy was very skinny and bony and he had freckles and blond hair and he must have been about six and a half feet tall. Leskov couldn't get himself up to look like that even if he had all the make-up in Hollywood!"

"How could you tell he had blond hair if he was wearing a hat?"

203

"I could see the color of the hair around his ears."

"How could you tell he was six and a half feet tall, if he was sitting down?"

"I don't believe this," muttered Fisher.

"Tell me! How could you tell he was so tall!"

"Because he had these great big long legs! His knees almost came up to the top of the back seat! What's wrong with you? Don't you believe me? Jesus, don't tell me you don't believe even me!"

"I don't know," said Bennett introspectively, after a pause. Then he turned and started to go to the bedroom.

"Where are you going?" said Fisher.

Without answering, Bennett went to the bedroom closet and got his gray flannel suit and laid it on the bed. He got a starched white shirt from the chest of drawers, and also a pair of black socks and a blue tie and laid them on the bed too. The clothes he already had on he removed and put on a chair, keeping on only his underclothes. He put on the starched shirt and the flannel trousers, then sat on the edge of the bed to put on the black socks.

Fisher stood in the doorway and watched in silence for a few minutes. "What are you doing?" he said at last.

"Sarah wants me to come over. She said I have to wear a suit. Can you drive me over there?"

"Sure," said Fisher and he turned around and went back into the livingroom and kneeled by his suitcase and started to rummage around in it.

Bennett got up quickly and went to the doorway. "What are you doing?" he said.

"I'm getting my suit . . . There . . . here we go!"
Fisher took out a dark blue suit on a hanger and held
it up proudly.

"Wait," said Bennett.

"What's wrong?"

"You don't have to . . . to put the suit on right
now . . . you won't need it until later . . . she doesn't
want people over right now . . . "

"I thought you said she had a house full of people."

"I don't know if it's a houseful. Maybe it's just a
few people. She said they were strangers. They're
probably from the funeral home."

"Then how come she wants you?"

"She just wants one person. To keep her company
for a while. Until the family gets there."

"Maybe two persons will be better. Look, if I pick
up that I'm in the way, I'll leave."

"Just give it a few hours, Fisher. What's the point
of making a scene? The woman just lost her husband,
for godsakes."

"I thought you said you don't believe her."

"I never said that. I was just talking about, like,
possibilities . . . "

"Then you do believe her."

"Well, I . . . mainly I do, yes . . . at any rate, I
don't disbelieve her."

"Forget it, I'm going," said Fisher resolutely and
he lay the suit on the chair and, kneeling again by
the suitcase, took out a pair of socks and began to
rummage around for some other things.

"You can't, dammit!" cried Bennett.

"Why? What's it to you?"

"She . . . she is under a lot of strain at the moment . . . "

"So are we all."

"Look, Fisher, she doesn't want you there."

"I thought you said it was just 'people' that she doesn't want."

"That's right."

"But she wants you, right?"

"Right."

"So that means you're not just people."

"Right."

"So? Neither am I!"

"Nobody is saying that you are. In fact, she probably would have called you except that she thought you'd left town."

"Exactly. But now she knows that I'm here, because I just spoke to her on your telephone, and if I don't go in and see her, she may think I don't care."

"She won't think that at all."

Fisher stood up. "How the hell do you know what she'll think! You don't have the faintest clue about her! You can't even make up your mind about whether or not she is just pretty little devoted caring Sarah who says what she means, or if she is some kind of a haunted nut-job who is running a weird con game on you!"

"Don't talk that way about her, Fisher."

"It's not me that's talking about her that way, it's you!"

"Look, dammit, she doesn't want you in the house!"

"Let me be the judge of that," said Fisher.

"There's nothing to judge! She was absolutely clear on the point! She does not want you in the house!

She said that if I let you in, she would never speak to me again!"

"What?"

"I'm sorry . . . I didn't mean . . . you . . . you pushed me to . . . to . . . "

"That little bitch . . . "

"Look, Fisher . . . she . . . she said you could come over later . . . in a few hours . . . just not right now . . . she just needs a little time . . . you see? . . . she . . . she likes you . . . there was nothing personal in it . . . honest . . . "

"Fine," said Fisher in a somber tone, and then he turned to gaze abstractly at the wall to his left, and his eyes filled with tears.

For a minute or so the two young men stood quite still. Then Fisher set about getting dressed. Slowly, like some fantastical liquid form moving through air, he dressed himself in the blue suit, with a starched white shirt, silver cufflinks, and a dark maroon woolen tie, which he knotted in a half-windsor without the help of a mirror.

Fisher said, "If Sarah changes her mind and invites me in, at least I'll be properly dressed."

"Jesus, Fisher."

"Just . . . just hold me for a minute . . . please . . . "

Bennett went and put his arms around Fisher and held him briefly, a trembling feminine body in the masculine suit, and then, embarrassed, moved away, to the window, and glanced out at the street.

"I know how difficult this must be for you," said Fisher after a moment.

"What?"

"Leskov . . . dying . . . I know how much you loved him . . . "

"Loved him!" said Bennett. "I hated him. I hated the son of a bitch. He was driving me nuts."

"There's no point in pretending anymore. What's the use? He's dead. It doesn't matter."

"What are you talking about? Are you crazy?"

"Look," Fisher said mysteriously, "I know."

"What the hell does that mean?"

"It means I know about the other night. So does Sarah."

Bennett paled with terror. "What other night?" he said.

"The other night when you and Leskov went drinking after the dress rehearsal."

"What do you know about it?"

"Everything. Leskov told me. And so did Steinmetz."

"Steinmetz! How the hell does Steinmetz know?"

"He said he was there."

"Where?"

"In the bar. Smitty's Place."

"I didn't see Steinmetz in any bar."

"He said you and he had a conversation there . . . about Norman Vincent Peale and the power of positive thinking."

"What did he say I said?"

"He just said that you were funny and that you made him laugh."

"Was Leskov with you when Steinmetz told you this?"

"No. Why?"

"Because maybe they cooked all this up . . . the whole story . . . between the two of them . . . just to play a little joke on you . . . "

"What do you mean by 'maybe'?" said Fisher. "Did this thing happen, or didn't it?"

"What exactly did Steinmetz tell you about what happened between me and Leskov?"

"The same thing that Leskov told me. That you made this big speech to Leskov, saying that you loved him . . . and that you kissed him . . . that you got up out of your chair and took Leskov's face in your hands and kissed him on the forehead and the cheek."

After a pause Bennett said, "And the mouth too?"

"They didn't say," said Fisher. "They just said that at the end you took his hands and kissed them too."

"They said I kissed his hands?"

"Yes. Isn't this true?"

"I think I'm going to be sick . . . "

"They said you went on with it a long time, and that you were saying the most extravagant things about him."

"What sort of things?"

"Praise . . . admiration . . . for his intelligence . . . his cleanliness . . . even the shape of his nose . . . "

"I never said such things, Fisher."

"You mean Leskov and Steinmetz both lied to me?"

"Use your head, for godsakes. Does any of this seem plausible to you? If any man ever carried on like that in Smitty's Place, he'd be thrown out on his ear."

"Actually, they said that you almost were . . . that at first all the oldtimers . . . the regulars . . . all those

old Swedes and Irish guys that work at the mill . . .
they were laughing like hell . . . cheering . . . making
obscene jokes . . . you know how those guys are . . .
and then they got so noisy and crazy, and the language
got so out of hand, that some middle-aged couple,
that man-and-wife team that are both clerks at the
bank and wear the same kind of eyeglasses and look
like twins . . . I forget their names . . . "

"Novotny."

"Mister and Missus Novotny, that's it . . . they
walked out in a huff. And then the bartender, the big
guy that they call Bazooka . . . Bazooka came out
from behind the bar and grabbed you and told you
that either you had to sit down and behave yourself,
or he was going to throw you out. Now, tell me, did
this happen, or didn't it?"

"What was Leskov doing while all this was going
on?"

"Steinmetz said that Leskov just sat there with this
big grin on his face . . . very composed . . . very
imperial . . . like some goddam sultan out of *The
Arabian Nights* . . . as if all this praise and admiration
and kissing of the hands were exactly what he had
coming to him and were the most natural thing in
the world . . . "

"Is that your word, or Steinmetz's?"

"Which word?"

"Sultan."

"Steinmetz."

Bennett said, "We have to go."

He went to the closet and got out a light beige
cotton coat that was called a raincoat by the manu-

210

facturer but in fact was not much use against rain. He put the coat on and went to the window and drew the curtains to have a look at the weather. The sun had not yet come up; or perhaps it had; it was hard to tell, for the sky was gray and flat like a sheet of stone in the east, and black and smoky in the west. Though it was not raining now, rain or even snow were not out of the question in such a sky, and he went back to the closet and got his umbrella.

Fisher said, "You can't do this to me."

"What am I doing to you?"

"You have got to talk."

"About what?"

"About is the story true, or isn't it."

"Which story?"

"The story about you and Leskov in Smitty's, dammit."

Bennett smiled nervously, then cast his eyes down. "I don't know," he said.

"You don't know?"

"No."

The two friends looked at each other in silence for a few moments.

Then Fisher said, "You don't remember." He said this flatly and with some tenderness.

"We have to get going," said Bennett rather weakly. ". . . really . . . I . . . Sarah is expecting me . . ."

"Right . . . right . . ." said Fisher, and immediately he went and got on his knees in front of his suitcase and shut it and latched it; then he stood up and said, "Ready to go."

As he took his suitcase by the handle and lifted it off the floor, he seemed, paradoxically, like a man who has just been relieved of a burden.

The two friends left the house and walked to the car.

Fisher went and opened the trunk and took out a raincoat, the style of which was identical to Bennett's; then he laid the suitcase in the trunk and shut the lid. As he was slipping into the raincoat, he suddenly became aware of Bennett's eyes gazing at him curiously.

"What's wrong?" said Fisher.

"Nothing," said Bennett, turning away in embarrassment.

Then he walked around the side of the car and got in the front seat.

A moment later Fisher also got in the front seat.

Fisher drove. He drove slowly and somewhat stiffly, sitting up straight and keeping both hands on the wheel.

After a minute or two of uneasy silence, Bennett said, "What else did Steinmetz tell you?"

"He didn't say much else."

"I need to know about this, Fisher."

"There isn't much more I can remember."

"You mean all he told you was I made this big scene at Smitty's, and he didn't tell you what happened afterward?"

"I don't think he knows what happened afterward."

"Why? Did he leave the bar at that point?"

"No. You did. You and Leskov. Steinmetz said that right at the peak, when the whole situation looked

212

like it might get out of hand, Leskov tried to calm you down, which, apparently, he did manage to some extent, and then he got the check and took you out of the place. Steinmetz said that at this point Leskov had this very concerned look on his face. 'Sober' was the word Steinmetz used. I remember that word, because he leaned on it and mentioned something about how much Leskov had been drinking."

"Did Steinmetz know anything about where Leskov and I went or what we did?"

"No."

"Did you ask him?"

"No. But I remember he said something like, 'God knows where the hell they went' . . . something like that."

"What about Leskov? You said that both Leskov and Steinmetz told you the same story. Didn't Leskov say anything about what happened afterward, or at least where he took me?"

"When Leskov told the story, he never mentioned the fact that he tried to calm you down, or that he took you out of the bar."

"Who told you the story first, Leskov or Steinmetz?"

"Steinmetz."

"So, then, when Leskov told you the story, you were hearing it for the second time, and you already knew that at the end he calmed me down and took me out of the bar."

"Right."

"So—weren't you curious?"

"Of course I was curious! And I did ask him about it. But for an answer he just gave me one of those nasty looks of his, which made me feel like I was a slimy gossip-hungry little bug, and I backed off."

"You should have pressed him, dammit."

After a pause Fisher said, "If I'd have been able to foresee that within the next twenty-four hours you on the one hand were going to be afflicted by an amnesiac episode, and Leskov on the other hand was going to die, no doubt I would have pressed him, but as matters stood I did not foresee anything of the kind, and so I kept my mouth shut."

The harsh pompous tone of this reproof brought Bennett up short, and he brooded in silence for a minute or so.

Then he said, "A few minutes ago you said that Steinmetz told you that last night in the bar he and I had a talk about Norman Vincent Peale and the power of positive thinking, and that Steinmetz said that I had been funny and made him laugh. Didn't you say that?"

"Yes. I did."

"Okay . . . now . . . I have to tell you that I don't remember this at all, this talk with Steinmetz, but I assume it must have taken place at some point in time *before* I told Leskov I loved and admired him, because *after* I did this, according to Steinmetz, I was immediately taken out of the place. Isn't that right?"

"Yes."

"So, then, the last thing I remember—which is a story, a horror story that Leskov told me about how his name got to be Leskov—this story did not lead straight to the love-and-admiration thing. There was something else in between. At any rate there was at

214

least this little talk with Steinmetz, and then, maybe, there could have been other things as well. Are you following this?"

"What was the story Leskov told you?"

"The main idea was that Leskov's father was born in Russia with a Hebrew name, and that one Easter Sunday, when he was twenty years old, his parents and sister were slaughtered by, I think, Cossacks . . . and that to protect his life, and to make a good escape from the country, he decided to hid his identity as a Jew, and so he got rid of his Hebrew name and took up the name Leskov . . . "

"Wait a minute. You mean Leskov is not a Jewish name?"

"Leskov is just Russian, a common Russian name."

"I always thought of Leskov as a Jewish name."

"So do a lot of people. That was one of the points of the story. At the end Leskov said that in this country a lot of people mistake Russian names for Jewish, and so in the end he and his family did not, as he put it, 'altogether escape the liabilities of a Jewish name—and this, naturally, gives him a certain twisted pleasure—and also it allows him to consider himself superior to me. Because nobody mistakes Bennett for a Jewish name, right? And he made some remark about that, about my name, and that is the last thing I remember, that remark about my name, and the way it got me."

"How did it get you?"

"It just got me, that's all. Can't you understand 'got'? It was like a hand around my throat, and inside my chest there was this pounding, like a hammer pounding on the wall of my chest, and I felt like either the hand was going to choke me to death, or the hammer was going to break my body into a thousand pieces like a clay pot."

"You were in a rage."

"Call it what you like. It doesn't matter. For me what matters is: how did I get from this hand-on-the-throat hammer-on-the-chest thing to . . . to this other thing, this thing where I got up and told Leskov I loved and admired him, right there in Smitty's place, in front of the Novotnys and Bazooka and all those roughneck barrelhouse fatfaced types from the mill!"

After a pause Fisher said, "Steinmetz said that when you first came over to his table, you scared him a little, because you looked angry, and that at first he supposed from the look on your face that you had come over to him to pick a fight."

"But I didn't, right? Instead he and I had this talk, this funny talk about Norman Vincent Peale, right?"

"Right. He said it was kind of weird. And then, after this talk about Norman Vincent Peale, you went straight back to Leskov and immediately launched into your . . . your speech . . . "

"Wait . . . wait!" said Bennett. "So, this is probably the sequence of events: First there was Leskov's horror story, then his remark about my name, then this hand-around-the-throat hammer-on-the-chest feeling, and then, right there, in the middle of this scary feeling, I got up, went over to Steinmetz, had the talk with him about Norman Vincent Peale, and then, without delay, went back to Leskov and told him I loved and admired him. Isn't that the way this all seems to have happened?"

216

"Well . . . yes. I suppose. Except that you can't be sure that it was right after the remark about your name that you went over to Steinmetz, though that would account for why you had an angry look on your face when you first came up to him."

"Right. But really the particular content of the remark makes no difference to the general scheme of things here, Fisher, because whenever you have a talk with Leskov, you can always count on plenty of remarks, and so the angry look on my face could just as well have been related to some other remark of his, and one that was just as rotten and oily and aggravating!

"But, then, still, it all seems very . . . very peculiar . . . because all these moves that I made in Smitty's place, they don't seem to have anything to do with one another. Do you see? If we take our version of the scene in Smitty's as the way things really happened, what do we have? We have a sort of picture of a set of moves I made, and the picture is clear enough, I suppose, but the moves themselves don't appear to lead from one to the other in any sensible way. One moment I am angry, and the next moment without any apparent provocation I am running over to Steinmetz and engaging him in some comic routine about Norman Vincent Peale, and then the next moment I am back to Leskov and telling him that I love and admire him . . . and, to top it all off, I am *tell*ing him this only a few minutes after he has insulted me! Do you see? None of this, actually, connects! Instead of going to Steinmetz and talking about Norman Vincent Peale, I might just as well have leaped up on the table and done a tap dance! Do you see what I am saying? I have this set of moves, and it makes a picture of some sort, but there is no . . . no sense to it all . . . because the moves don't really connect. Which makes the whole business very hard to swallow. And so, Fisher, I don't think we have a correct picture of what really happened."

"Why?"

"I just told you! Because these moves of mine don't really in any ordinary human way have anything to do with one another. You see? They . . . they don't connect!"

"Maybe that's the point," said Fisher cautiously.

"What are you saying?"

"I'm saying that maybe the picture is, in fact, correct, and that these moves of yours were, in fact, unconnected. Look, have you ever seen someone behave like that? It can be . . . very unsettling . . . even for someone as self-possessed as Leskov. And maybe that is why Leskov seemed to be so concerned, and why he took you out of the bar."

With this Fisher lapsed into silence, apparently waiting for an answer, but none came; after two or three minutes had gone by, he asked, "What do you think?"

"I don't know," said Bennett quietly. "Mainly I think that what you say is plausible, very plausible . . . but, frankly, Fisher, it's kind of hard to take. Can you understand that?"

During the remaining mile or so of the drive the two friends did not speak again, until they pulled up at the curb in front of Leskov's apartment.

Then Fisher said, "I'll wait for you."

"I may be in there for hours," said Bennett.

"Just go in and take a quick look, and then come out and tell me if he is really dead."

"I thought I was the one with the doubts."

"You were. But doubt is contagious. And anyway, when you are dealing with Leskov, your motto should always be: Remember the lawn chairs."

Bennett frowned. After a moment he said, "I can't just run in and look at the body and run out again. Everybody will think I'm a lunatic."

"In that case, take your time. I'm in no rush."

"Give me about half an hour."

"Take an hour. I have *Anna Karenina* in the glove compartment and the *New York Times* crossword puzzle under the seat."

Bennett got out of the car and walked up the path slowly, with his hands in the pockets of his coat, his eyes on the ground. Just as his foot touched the doorstep, the door opened from within, and Sarah appeared in the doorway, her eyes and nose and mouth bruised and swollen with grief.

"What took you so long?" she said, and before he had time to answer, she drew him inside and shut the door and threw her arms around him, resting the side of her face on his chest, and said, "I'm so glad you're here."

Nine bearded men in black suits and black hats stood in the livingroom. They stood in three groups of three, engaged in solemn intense discussion in an undertone in Yiddish. Out of the corners of their eyes they glanced at Bennett and Sarah suspiciously. Many black overcoats were piled on the sofa, and one coat, the only one with a Persian lamb collar, was draped over a chair. At the far end of the room the door to the main bedroom was open. Candles were burning in the bedroom. On the bed lay a body under a dark yellow sheet. Here and there about the room were still more bearded men in black suits and black hats, sitting on bridge chairs. They had books in their hands. Their heads were bowed to the books, and their lips were moving. In the air was a faint smell of incense. The candlelight created grotesque animated shadows in the room, and it was hard to tell precisely how many men were in there. It may have been only four or five, or as many as ten.

"Come and talk to me over here," said Sarah in a hushed voice, taking Bennett by the hand and leading him to a corner of the room near the front window. "Alice should be here any minute, and I want to keep an eye out and catch her before she rings the bell and wakes up Annie. I want Annie to sleep as late as she can, and the doorbell has a very nasty sound and always wakes her. God knows what I'm going to tell her when she does wake. Dimitri said that I should tell her that her Daddy has gone to Heaven to live with the angels, and that she should pray for him and be glad for him, glad that he is with the angels, and that he will always love her and be watching her, and that one day another man will come and be her Daddy, and that he will be a very good man, who will live a very long time, until she is a grown-up lady, and that she will love him very much. Dimitri was wonderful with stories, just wonderful, and Annie was always asking him to tell her another one, usually about something that frightened her, but I don't know if I can bring it off as well as he used to. Yesterday she asked him to tell her a story about the thunder, which he did, but I don't know how successful he was, because we haven't had any more thunder since then. I know I am rattling on, David, but you will have to forgive me. In any case, my guess is that the child will be less disturbed by the death of her father than by all these strange men with their big beards and bushy eyebrows and black suits. She's never before seen men like these, and to find so many of them all over the place the minute she wakes up is bound to give her a bad turn, don't you think? What can I tell her about them? Maybe I ought just to follow along the line of the other story and tell her that these men are special men . . . special men who know special prayers that will help her Daddy get to Heaven, so that he can be with the angels. Yes, I think that will be just the thing. As soon as she wakes up, I will go in and tell her about her Daddy, and then I will tell her about the men in black suits that she will see when she comes out to the livingroom, and then I'll dress her and pack her off with Alice for the day. Alice can take her in the Buick and go to the luncheonette . . . or wherever she wants . . . Alice is very good with her . . . God, where is that woman! I do wish she would hurry! If Annie wakes up before Alice gets here, I just don't know what I am going to do. Oh, look, Jimmy's Plymouth is still out there. What's he doing? It looks like he is reading a book.

Don't tell me that he is sitting out there in the cold waiting for you. I hope not. Because I intend to keep you here for a while . . . "

"No, no, he just was . . . worried. He wanted me to make sure that . . . that you were all right before he takes off. He wanted me to come in and make sure that you were all right, you see, and I promised that I would come in and see, and then come out and let him know . . . also he wanted me to ask you if you need any shopping done . . . "

"Oh, God, now you've made me feel so terribly guilty. You didn't tell him what I said about him, did you?"

"No, no, of course not."

"Because I wouldn't want to hurt Jimmy for all the world. He is so . . . so fragile . . . and sensitive . . . and, really, he has a very good heart. It's just that right now I need to be just a little selfish and try to keep my wits . . . so that I don't frighten Annie . . . I need to be able to reassure her . . . and I don't want to be distracted at the moment by . . . by silly things . . . do you know what I am talking about? Jimmy had a very strong attraction to Dimitri that was positively physical . . . you could just feel it in the air . . . and it used to make me sometimes want to jump out of my skin . . . Just go on out and tell him that I am fine, fine, and that I don't need any shopping done . . . but that I said thank you . . . thank you very much . . . and . . . and that I will see him later . . . at the funeral . . . the funeral is to be at four-thirty this afternoon . . . he can get the details later from you . . . I'll write them down for you . . . please go now . . . I can't bear to think of him sitting out there in the cold another minute . . . "

"There's no hurry. I told him that I would be at least half an hour . . . besides, he has a heater in the car and a good book . . . he's perfectly content . . . and anyway first I want to go and look at . . . that is, pay my respects to . . . to Dimitri . . . and . . . and see him one last time . . . "

"Oh, no, no, you can't do that, David."

"Why not?"

"Because all these men here won't let you. Exhibiting the body is absolutely forbidden by Jewish custom. Don't you know that? A fine Jew you are. Well, I know that at some funerals with a modern rabbi the body is shown, but these men here are not modern . . . They are very orthodox, very strict . . . Dimitri was crazy about them . . . every morning he used to get up before dawn and go down to that little *shul* they have behind the shoe repair shop in the village . . . have you ever been in there? When he was alive, I wasn't supposed to tell anyone about this, but now I suppose it's all right, isn't it? He used to go there and pray and study . . . he loved all those tedious old arguments about cows and debts and whether you should walk on the left side of this or the right side of that . . . and there is one old man, the one with the red beard over in the corner—do you see him?— that is Berel Yakov—he is an expert on Cabala—the past three months Dimitri was studying with him— every day Dimitri would come home with a funny story about Berel Yakov—Dimitri used to call him

223

The Magician—'Do you know what The Magician said today?'—I never understood these stories or why Dimitri thought they were so funny—but it used to give me pleasure to hear them—does that sound too stupid of me? What I liked about the Berel Yakov stories was the way Dimitri used to light up when he told them—he'd get just like a young boy, and then usually he would end up making the most passionate love to me—but with such a light heart—so . . . so playful!—do you know what I am talking about? Oh, God, I shouldn't be saying these things . . . "

She began to weep. From a pocket in her dress, she took a white handkerchief and wiped her eyes and her nose.

Bennett stood very still. At a loss for what to say or do, he simply gazed at her stupidly, scarcely daring to breathe.

After a moment she looked up with a faint smile. "It was so . . . so good of you to come here, David . . . you can't possibly know how much it means to me to have you here right now . . . and . . . and that is a very, very handsome suit . . . I do like that suit very much . . . I don't think I've ever seen you in a suit before . . . you ought to wear it more often . . . it . . . it suits you! . . . oh my, sorry . . . that really is a very flabby pun, isn't it . . . if Dimitri were to have heard me say it to you, he would not let me get away with it without a terrible groan . . . he did used to love to groan at my puns . . . great big groans . . . and then we'd laugh . . . laugh and laugh . . . and then, when we stopped laughing, he would get this most hopelessly dismal melancholy look

on his face as if all the world were lost . . . lost
forever . . . and then he'd shake his head in despair
and . . . and repeat the pun . . . and we'd start
laughing all over again! . . . Oh, David, I do miss
him horribly . . . he's been gone only two hours, and
already I miss him! . . . horribly, horribly . . . I
honestly don't know how I am going to go on without
him . . . but I must, mustn't I . . . for Annie . . .
What would you say if suddenly you were to find that
I had become a very observant, very orthodox Jewish
lady? . . . that I had shaved my head and got a wig,
and a long black dress, and big clumsy shoes, and
two sets of dishes, and a kerchief . . . all of it . . .
what would you say? . . . would you laugh? . . .
would you be happy for me? . . . would you be sad?
. . . would you think that I had made a mistake?
. . . would you think that I was merely playing a
trick on myself to avoid the grief of losing Dimitri?
. . . Oh, God, look what I am doing to you . . .
please forgive me, David . . . you don't have to answer
such questions . . . I myself can't answer them . . .
because . . . because . . . because I don't myself know
what I would think about such a state of affairs . . .
all I know is that it would be a way to feel that I
was still close to Dimitri . . . a few months ago I
told Dimitri that if he would like it, I would keep a
kosher home, and . . . and try to be a real Jewish
wife . . . keep the Sabbath . . . everything . . . just
like the wives of all these men . . . that I would go
to the rabbi's wife and talk to her and ask her to
teach me . . . but Dimitri wouldn't hear of it . . .
'What would I want with a woman like that?' he said.

225

'A woman like that would drive me crazy!' All the same, I know he was touched by the offer . . . because later in the day he brought me two dozen lilacs and six orchids that must have cost a fortune and were arranged in the most exquisite bouquet . . . and also he brought a big fresh ham from the A&P—which he roasted himself—he put slices of pineapple on it and served it with beans and sauerkraut—for dessert there was strawberry ice cream . . . well, Dimitri was always full of surprises . . . I never knew what he was going to come up with . . . and this was very difficult at times, believe me, but also continually exciting, and I wouldn't have wished him to be different in any way—some people, like Olive, for example, and poor simple Steinmetz, thought that Dimitri was an absolutely insane and evil person—you don't know how many times I have received offers of sympathy from such people, when sympathy was really the last thing I wished for . . . what I really wished for was that everyone should envy me—envy my happiness—my good luck—envy me for having such a husband—and it used to make me sad—unspeakably sad, David!— that such people were so blind . . . so unappreciative . . . of . . . of him! Of course, I realize that it was perfectly natural that such people should have such a view of Dimitri . . . but they are very, very irksome to me, all the same . . . Why are you smiling? Do you think I am being silly?"

Bennett took Sarah's hand.

"Here she comes," he said, meaning to alert Sarah's attention to the window and the arrival of Alice, who

226

had just crossed the road in front of the house and was making her way up the walk to the door.

But Sarah ignored the window, continuing to look in Bennett's eyes, and tightened her grip on his hand.

In a moment the doorbell rang, and she gave a start. The men in black suits quieted abruptly and frowned at the door.

"Damn," she said, hurrying to the door. "I told Alice not to ring that thing."

She opened the door and, frowning, said in a whisper, "Come in, come in . . . "

"Oops," said Alice, putting one hand over her mouth. "I wasn't supposed to ring the bell, was I."

"I do wish you hadn't," said Sarah. "But, really, it's my fault. I meant to watch for you, and I . . . I just got distracted for a moment. The main thing, though, is that you've come . . . it's really very good of you . . . and I do so need your help at the moment. Just go in and check on Annie, will you? If she's awake, signal me at the door, and I'll come in and talk to her. Otherwise please just sit in her room until she wakes, will you? I don't want her waking up and walking into all this until I've had a chance to prepare her a little. I've left a few magazines and books in a pile by the chair, and you can turn on the little lamp. It's quite a good reading lamp, and usually it doesn't wake her. I'll bring you a cup of coffee in five minutes . . . or would you prefer tea?"

"Coffee is fine," said Alice, glancing furtively at Bennett.

"Hi, Alice," he said softly.

Alice blushed, cast her eyes down, and then, without giving a reply to Bennett's greeting, made her way

227

through the bearded men in black suits, with an exaggerated girlish deference, scarcely daring to look at them, except surreptitiously out of the corners of her eyes.

"I suppose I should have introduced her to some of these men," said Sarah. "Would that have been the proper thing to do? Oh, I . . . I just don't know . . . I don't know what exactly is expected of me . . . Do you have some idea about this, David? I really don't want to offend any of these men—really, I don't—but they do have these very peculiar ideas about women, you know."

"Maybe you should just ask them about it," said Bennett.

"Oh, my . . . I almost forgot!" said Sarah, putting one hand on her forehead. Then she reached into a large pocket in her dress and took out a piece of notepaper folded in half, and handed it to Bennett.

"What's this?" he said.

"Dimitri left it for you. Once he gave up on your getting here in time, he asked for a piece of paper and a fountain pen, and he scribbled this little note. He said it was very important, and that I should give it to you the moment you arrived—and then . . . then I forgot! How could I forget a thing like that? He made me promise not to read it, but . . . but I'm afraid I did, David . . . will you forgive me? As it turns out, I really don't think I've been intrusive, because, honestly, I don't understand the note at all."

Bennett unfolded the notepaper and saw in the flourish of Leskov's grand unmistakable script only an address, a time, and an exclamation point.

228

"What time is it?" said Bennett.

"I don't know," said Sarah, "There's a clock in the kitchen . . . David, what is that address?"

"Just a minute," said Bennett, and he crossed the livingroom and approached one of the bearded men, who was wearing a wristwatch on a brown leather band.

"Excuse me . . . could you please tell me what time it is?"

"Eh?"

"The time," repeated Bennett, tapping his own wrist as a pantomime gesture to reinforce his meaning.

"Ah!" said the bearded man, apparently delighted with the question. "The time! Yes, yes. The time is . . . is ten . . . no, no . . . nine . . . actually just a little more than nine minutes after seven . . . on Bulova time. Berel Yakov."

"Excuse me?"

"Berel Yakov. My name." He offered his hand.

Bennett took Berel Yakov's hand. "I am very pleased to meet you."

"Likewise." Berel Yakov applied a very gentle pressure on Bennett's hand and then let go and said, "And your name?"

Bennett paused a moment, then gave his Hebrew name.

The name apparently delighted Berel Yakov, and he at once introduced the other two bearded men he had been engaged in discussion with before Bennett had interrupted.

229

The other two bearded men smiled broadly, also clearly pleased with the name that Bennett had identified himself with, and they too offered their hands, each applying the same gentle pressure as had Berel Yakov.

"You are a relative of . . . " Here Berel Yakov mentioned another Hebrew name.

After a moment's reflection Bennett realized that this other name referred to Leskov.

"No, no," said Bennett. "We were . . . friends."

"Ah, friends, yes. I am sorry. It is hard to lose a friend. Specially when you are so young. And when the friend you lost also was so young. And of such a fine character! So intelligent! It is a great loss for all of us. We too were friends."

"Could you please tell me the time again?"

"The time? With pleasure. Here. Eleven minutes after seven exactly. You have an appointment?"

"Yes, yes, excuse me . . . "

Bennett walked back into the bedroom, which was dimly lit only by candlelight. There were five candles. As soon as he stepped into the room, the bearded men—there were about ten—looked up from their books and grew silent, and three of them stood up and offered their hands. No words were exchanged, no names offered by way of introduction, only the hands, and then a chair too was offered, by all three bearded men acting in concert; but Bennett declined, not with words, only with a deferential gesture, after which he turned to look for a moment at the body of Leskov, visible in vague outline under the yellow sheet. As being near the body for a moment was all

230

he had come in for in the first place, he then turned away abruptly, and with a fleeting, perhaps uncomprehended gesture of apology to the three bearded men, who in concert had offered him a chair, he went out of the room.

At the front door, he was given another piece of notepaper by Sarah.

"This is the time and place of the funeral, David," she said. "Please, please be there. It is in a little cemetery about five miles from here. If you need a ride, come here first and drive over with me. I'm going to leave at about three."

"I'll be here."

"Thank you . . . thank you so much, David . . . " Tears filled her eyes, and she put her arms around him and held him close to her and wept on his shoulder quietly for a minute or two.

He loved her, he thought.

When she let him go, she said, "You're going to that address, aren't you."

"Yes."

"Are you going to tell me what it is? Later? When you find out?"

"Yes."

"You're late, though. I checked the clock in the kitchen."

Bennett examined her eyes for a trace of guile, but finding none, he took her hand and held it gently a moment, then let go and stepped out onto the doorstep and hurried down the path to the Plymouth.

"Well?" said Fisher as soon as Bennett had settled himself in the front seat and shut the door.

"Take me to 1311 Elm, Fisher. Do you know where that is?"

"Is he dead?"

"Yes."

"You saw the body?"

"I saw as much of it as I could. It was under a sheet."

"Then you're convinced."

"Let me put it this way, Fisher. If Leskov is not really dead, then there are fifteen Hasidic Jews in that apartment, or fifteen actors disguised as Hasidic Jews, plus two apparently sane honest women, who are collaborating in one of the most melancholy deceptions ever perpetrated on a graduate fellow of the humanities in this decade. Now, please, if you know the way, take me to 1311 Elm as fast as you can."

"Why?"

"Just do it, Fisher. I'll tell you on the way."

"I've got a few questions first, dammit."

"Do you know the way?"

"Yes."

"Then start driving, and I promise I'll answer every question you have. Please, Fisher . . . it's important!"

Fisher examined Bennett's face a moment, then started the engine and guided the Plymouth onto the road.

"Can you step it up a bit?" said Bennett.

"As soon as we get onto Forest Hill Road, I'll step it up. It's about a ten-minute drive, so relax. Now, tell me what is this about fifteen Hasidic Jews?"

"Apparently Leskov used to pray with them every morning."

"You're kidding."

"No. Also he used to study with them. He left instructions that they should take care of the funeral."

"How does Sarah feel about that?"

"She's a little confused, but she accepts it."

"Weird," declared Fisher thoughtfully, after a pause.

"Maybe. But it will spare a lot of expense. The Hasids around here are quite poor, and they like a simple funeral in any case. A rough pine coffin, and the body has to be in the ground within the day. There won't be any cost for a funeral home, or for any extras at all. A box, a piece of ground, and a prayer, and that will be the end of it."

"How do you know about all this?"

"I went to Hebrew school a few hours a week when I was a kid. My parents rejected all the trappings of religion themselves, but they sent me to Hebrew school because it was what they thought they were obliged to do. Don't ask me why."

"I'm not staying for the funeral."

"Why not? You won't have to hang around much longer. It will be this afternoon at four, and it will be over in half an hour. You could be back on the road before dark."

"Forget it. I'm going to drop you off and get going. I could be in New Hampshire before morning. If I stay around, I'm asking for trouble. Olive is bound to go to the funeral just to make sure that Leskov is really out of the picture. If I'm there, she'll make a scene right at the grave, believe me, and I'm not up to it. I loved Leskov, man, and I respected him too, and I don't want to be the one responsible for provoking a comic opera at his last rites. He deserves better. Can you understand that?"

"Yes," said Bennett.

"What is this address I'm taking you to?"

"1311 Elm."

"I meant, what is there?"

"It's just . . . it's a . . . I have to run an errand for the Hasids—something to do with the funeral arrangements . . . there are certain things they need for the funeral."

"What kind of things?"

"Just . . . like . . . certain books . . . ritualistic objects . . . it's all very esoteric—just forget it, Fisher. My turn to ask a question. Is it really true that you and Leskov . . . you know . . . that you . . . "

"That we had something physical?"

"Yes."

"What do you think?"

"Don't ask me that," said Bennett. "At the moment every wheel in my brain is spinning in mud and the only thing I can think about is food! Do you realize I haven't eaten a proper meal in about thirty-six hours? I had some pretzels and chips at the party, but mainly I've been living on coffee—coffee, coffee, coffee!"

"Do you want to stop at the diner?"

"No, forget it. I don't have time for that right now."

"Well, anyway . . . it wasn't true."

"What wasn't true?"

"That Leskov and I had something physical. I just made that up . . . to get you angry . . . I'm sorry . . . "

234

As the Plymouth pulled up in front of 1311 Elm, Fisher said, "Will you be able to get a ride? Are you sure you don't want me to stay and give you a lift back?"

"I may be in there a while. I don't want you to have to wait around. Patience has a limit, and you have your own problems. I'll be all right. It's only a ten-minute walk from here to the campus, and I want to drop by the theater and help Dicataldo strike the set. He asked for volunteers last night, and probably not too many people will turn up. I wouldn't feel right if he ended up having to do the whole job by himself."

"I wouldn't leave here, if you . . . and I . . . if . . ."

"Write as soon as you have an address, okay? You're important to me, Fisher, and I don't want to lose touch with you. Don't look so blue. Why do you look so blue?"

"I suppose I should say it's because Leskov is dead, but that isn't it at the moment."

"Maybe you should stay and go to the funeral, Fisher. Funerals are important."

After a pause, Fisher said, "I'll write."

Bennett got out of the Plymouth and shut the door, then ducked his head to peer in the window. "Just be sure and write, okay?" he said.

Fisher nodded, gazing abstractly at the windshield.

1311 was a small three-story redbrick apartment building.

Bennett went in and looked at the mailboxes in the entry. The name on 4A was I. Horvath. Bennett knew nobody by this name. There appeared to be twelve apartments in all, four on each floor. He went through a small lobby and back through a dim corridor to the rear, where he found 4A stenciled on the last door. On the doorpost was a small buzzer, which he tapped briefly. Almost at once the door was opened by a short sickly man, whom Bennett recognized with some astonishment as the old man who owned the laundromat.

"You're late," he said wearily, with a frown, then stepped aside to let Bennett in.

Bennett walked past the old man into a dim foyer floored with stained linoleum.

The old man locked two locks and slipped the doorchain into its latch and said, "In there, in there!" with an impatient gesture, indicating that Bennett should go through the doorway to the right, instead of the doorway to the left, which at first he had begun to turn into.

The doorway to the right opened onto a medium-sized room, rather dark and dirty, and crowded with various kinds of old worn furniture—beds, sofas, chairs, tables, even a stove and a sink—and all disarranged at odd angles, so that it was impossible to tell if the room were intended as a bedroom, a livingroom, or a kitchen. In fact, the room had the look more of a storage room than of anything else and reminded Bennett actually a little of the storage attic in his parents' house in Long Island, except that his parents' attic had a damp musty smell, as of moss and wet wood, whereas here the smell was of urine and something like boiled cabbage and decayed fish.

236

In a bed against the far wall lay an old woman.

"So, he's dead?" said the old man, coming out of the foyer at Bennett's back.

"Yes," said Bennett automatically, though startled by the question.

"You hear, Margaret? Your Dimitri has passed away!"

A groan issued from the old woman, and also some words, muttered in a foreign tongue.

"Come, come," said the old man, taking Bennett by the arm and urging him across the room. "We haven't got all day. My wife is a little suspicious of you, but don't let that bother you. I tell you this only to prepare you. At first she was suspicious of Dimitri too, but then in time, a week or two, she was crazy about him. Look who is here, Margaret. The fine young man you met yesterday. Dimitri's young friend. Look how good-looking he is! Ah, Margaret, don't turn your face to the wall. Look at the young man who has come to help us!"

Having made his way through the room as through a labyrinth, guided by the old man, Bennett now stood beside the bed, gazing at the old woman, who lay on her side, turned to the wall. Though her back was to him, he had enough height to see the profile of her face, which was swollen with purple boils here and there and scarred with tiny lesions on her forehead and chin. He judged her to be rather short, perhaps an inch or two above five feet, and to weigh at least twice as much as what ordinarily even a stout woman her size might weigh. On the side of her neck was a white bandaid. She was dressed in a brown flannel nightgown, over which was a sort of jacket, a woolen jacket in red and black plaid, such as is commonly associated with lumberjacks and millworkers. Around her head was tied a green kerchief, but the top of her head was exposed, revealing that her hair had fallen out in patches, so that only a few gray wisps remained.

At the foot of the bed stood a wheelchair, which the old man brought around to the side of the bed.

"The chair is here, Margaret," he said. "Come roll over a little. The young man is going to help us now to move you into the chair . . . " Then he added in a whisper, leaning close to Bennett, "Forgive me . . . I forget your name."

"David."

"David . . . yes, good. His name is David, Margaret. David is going to help us. Well, she isn't going to roll over. You see? What you have to do, then, is put your hands under her armpits and pull her over here to the chair. Are you strong enough to manage this?"

Bennett leaned across the bed and took hold of the old woman as he had been instructed and then tried to drag her away from the wall and across the bed toward the chair. She was very heavy, and she could do nothing with her body either to resist or to help, and her shoulders were trembling.

"Don't cry, Margaret. Why are you crying, you silly girl? Look how this young David is trying to help you. Come, give him a smile, my darling. What will he think of us? He will think, 'Why is Margaret crying? Maybe her husband abuses her.' You see? Then you will give me a bad reputation in the laundromat, and nobody will come and wash clothes there anymore, and then how will I make money? And what will we eat? Ah, there, now you have it, David. Now, into the chair. Can you manage it? I will hold the chair . . . there, easy, easy, gently, gently . . . that's it . . . very gently or you will bruise her . . . the slightest little bump and she starts to bleed . . . very good, very good . . . ah, good, you are very strong—see how strong he is, Margaret? Much stronger than his friend Dimitri. Your friend Dimitri, he was a good man, but he used to have such a hard time—he would huff and puff and . . . ah, it was pathetic . . . it used to take him sometimes ten minutes to get her from one side of the bed to the other. Remember, Margaret? And now, look at this: in two minutes already David has put you in the chair! Isn't that wonderful? Come, now we will take you to the window, and you can look at your lovely trees. Come, David, help me push her to the window."

With the old man's guidance, Bennett pushed the wheelchair through a maze of furniture to the window.

"Good, good, David. Everything else I can do myself—the bedpan, the clothing, the washing of the face and hands, the medication—all this is very simple. Come, come, I will talk to you in the foyer for a minute, eh? You can talk for a minute?"

Put off and puzzled by the incongruity of the old man's radical sadism in the laundromat and his clownish gallantry at home, Bennett said hardly a word in the foyer, but listened with wary attention, trying to piece together the information that was important to him, while the old man talked at a great rate.

Apparently one day about six months ago the old man and Leskov had struck up a conversation in the laundromat, and the old man had begun to complain about his problem of getting his wife from the bed to the wheelchair in the morning. As he himself was unable to manage the task, he had hired various people to help, but none had proved reliable; there would always be one or two days each week when they would turn up a few hours late, or not at all, and not only would this cause his wife terrible suffering, but also he would have to stay with her until he found other help, and sometimes this took hours and kept him from opening the laundromat for half the morning.

On hearing the old man's complaint, Leskov had volunteered for the job without hesitation, and, true to his word, never missed a single morning or turned up even a minute late in six months. This superb reliability, as far as the old man was concerned, was the essential thing. "Leskov," he said, "was like the sun!"—a comparison which startled Bennett, who never would have thought to compare Leskov to so bright an object.

From ten-thirty until evening, the old woman was attended by "someone from the agency," so in these hours the old man had no difficulty, for even when the regular attendant from the agency failed to show up, the agency always sent a replacement. What precisely this agency was, the old man did not say, and Bennett did not ask.

He did ask, however, what time he and Leskov had arrived the previous morning, and the old man replied that they had arrived at six-forty-five, which was a little earlier than usual.

"And," he added without prompting, "at five minutes after seven you left. Why do you ask?"

At this moment a groan issued from the other room, and he cocked his head to one side and clasped his hands.

"She wants me," he said, retreating obsequiously from the vestibule. "But in two minutes I'll be back, so, please, don't go away! Two minutes!"

As soon as Bennett was left alone, he began to try to sort out the new information. If he and Leskov had arrived here yesterday at six-forty-five, then what had they done before that? That is, what had they done between the time they left Smitty's bar and the time they arrived here at 1311 Elm? To Bennett's mind, the best theory was that they had driven around aimlessly in the Buick and talked, for there was nothing that Leskov had liked better than to drive around aimlessly and talk. A more definitive answer Bennett could not expect in this lifetime; however, he could expect, from various people who had seen him at Smitty's, a fair estimate of the time he and Leskov had left, and in this prospect lay the compensatory hope of assessing, if not the breadth of the theoretical talk, then at least its length. In any event, it was clear that at six-forty-five they arrived here at 1311 Elm, and that at five minutes after seven they left—which meant that Bennett might have been home and in bed and even fast asleep before seven-thirty, in which case, as it had been just before nine when he was awakened by the thunderstorm—the rain pouring through the open window, and so on—he would have slept only about an hour-and-a-half; which, finally, would account in part for why he had been in a disoriented state of mind all morning, and also for why, directly on his return from his trip to the laundromat, he had gotten back into bed and slept through the entire afternoon.

On the old man's reappearance in the vestibule, Bennett, supposing that he had now learned all he was likely to learn from this quarter, announced that he had an urgent appointment and would have to be going.

"Yes, yes, forgive me," said the old man. "I should not keep you. After all, you have your life, your studies. But there is just one more thing. It is only a little thing, and I wouldn't mention it, except that . . . how shall I say? . . . you see, Dimitri, he got into the habit after a while of fixing my wife a cup of tea. Lipton tea in a bag. Strong. With two lumps of sugar. And he used to bring it to her in the wheelchair and sit and talk with her for maybe five, ten minutes, no more. Of course, this is not absolutely required. I myself can fix the tea. Also I can sit and talk, even more than ten minutes. For me, if you come every morning at seven and take her from the bed to the chair, as you promised, this is enough."

"Maybe tomorrow," said Bennett. "Right now I have to . . . to . . . "

"Who says 'now'? I don't even say 'tomorrow.' Maybe in a few days, a week . . . two weeks . . . you see? I tell you only so that you should know that if you see a box of teabags on the shelf over the stove, and you want to make a cup of tea, nobody will stop you!"

242

As Bennett hurried through the damp cold tree-lined suburban streets, making his way to the college, turning right at the first corner, left at the next, and then right again at the next, and straight ahead for another eight blocks, he could not help thinking, somewhat obsessively, and with considerable irritation, about the old man's words, "as you promised," which, admittedly, and to the old man's credit, had been spoken without special emphasis. All the same, thought Bennett, emphasis or no emphasis, the words had been spoken, he had heard them, and . . . he was convinced! He had promised! This was clear. But was he obliged to keep a promise that he could not remember making? And if he did keep it, or try to keep it, how well really could he do this thing that he had promised to do? He was not Dimitri Leskov, after all. He was David Bennett. And being David Bennett, he was not accustomed to getting up at such an early hour, at least not ritualistically. And then, what about the tea? Undeniably, he had made no promise about the tea. The old man had been quite definite on this point. Bennett could make the tea, or not make the tea. Still, in either case, once he was there, in the apartment, the box of teabags would be there too, standing on the shelf and waiting for a decision. In short, one thing led to another. The promise led to the wheelchair, the wheelchair led to the tea, and the tea led to the talk. And then what? What would the talk lead to? And where would all this stop! Unquestionably, he ought to stop with the wheelchair, for the tea seemed to entail the talk, and even though he might manage the tea, how would he manage the talk? What would he say to this woman? Leskov was practiced in talking to all sorts of people, but Bennett was not. Moreover, he had no wish to talk to this woman. No doubt Leskov had wished to talk to her, and so of course he talked to her. But then Leskov had peculiar inclinations and had always wanted to talk to everybody. But did that mean that Bennett had to have the same inclinations? How could he be faulted for having different inclinations? Besides, what state of mind must he have been in yesterday to have committed himself to this project to begin with! Not the state of mind he was in today; that was certain! If he were to be true to himself, in fact, he would summon up his courage and go and confess that he had made a mistake and remove himself from the whole burdensome exercise altogether, and at once. He would visit the laundromat this morning, as soon as possible, and, looking directly in the old man's eyes, say that he was sorry, that he had made a mistake, that he would not be able to do this thing, and that somebody else, somebody more suitable, would have to be enlisted for the job. That was the way to go about it. After all, what were this old man and this old woman to Bennett? They were not family; they were hardly even casual acquaintances; they were nothing to him, nothing, and he was in no way in their debt. In the last analysis, considering the circumstances under which his original promise had been made, who could possibly have blamed him for having second thoughts? Nobody!

A few yards inside the perimeter of the campus, beside the black tarmac road that led to the theater, there were a bank of public telephones, and Bennett stopped to place a call to his parents, judging that he would be just in time to catch them before they left for work. The father was the first to come on the line, and then a moment later the mother picked up an extension in another room. Though Bennett had been prepared to assume an apologetic posture, anticipating that his parents would be worried about him, they turned out in fact not to be worried at all, except in the usual general way, and did not even bother to question him about where he had been or what he had done the previous night. Mainly they seemed concerned only to let him be advised of their annoyance with Sarah, insofar as she had waked them out of a sound sleep. Anxious to defend her, Bennett was quick to say, on Sarah's behalf, that her husband had just died last night, and this diverted his parents' annoyance at once, and even elicited from them a certain formal sympathy, though it was evident in their tone that, death or no death, whether Sarah had the right to wake up two perfect strangers at three in the morning was, from the moral point of view, still open to question.

This pious disengagement of theirs, quite naturally, struck Bennett as unjust, also as ferocious, and his heart began to pound in his throat, and irresistably there began to course through his mind the disorderly passionate scene he was supposed to have created in Smitty's bar the night before last in the company of Leskov, or at any rate Fisher's account of that scene, whereon, all at once, both to his own and his parents' amazement, he found himself talking about his bicycle.

The bicycle, or rather the theft of the bicycle, was a thing he had meant to talk about from the outset, by way of an excuse for his arriving home late last night, but clearly his parents were indifferent to his coming home late, so to offer them an excuse now seemed to him altogether beside the point; all the same, as he could not bring himself to speak of the deeper concerns pressing him, and the story of the bicycle was ready to hand and even had a certain intrinsic interest, once he had brought it up, he let himself go on with it at length; but then, getting caught up in a narrative excitement beyond his control, he soon found himself making the astonishing declaration that instead of buying a new bike, he was going to buy a used car! He didn't know what sort of car just yet, he said, but he had over three hundred dollars saved out of the grant money from last semester, and he was sure he could get something decent. He would go over to the used car lot in the village this afternoon and see what was available. He wanted something right away, today, something that would be good in the snow, for any minute now the snow would arrive, and he wanted to be prepared, not like last year, when the heavy winter weather had rendered his bike useless for over four months, and he had ended up having to walk nearly everywhere.

A car was just the thing, commented his mother agreeably, for maybe with a car he would go out more often and have some fun once in a while and get away from that gloomy apartment of his and those disgusting novels; but stay away from Chevies and Fords, put in the father, because their bodies were cheap and tinny and the doors and fenders were bound to fall off on the first bump; at which point an exceptionally musical operator in the alto range interrupted the circuit and said please to deposit another sixty-five cents for the next five minutes.

In an attempt to get in a last word to his parents, Bennett raised his voice over a new hum on the line to say that he had no more change; he waited a moment or two for a reply, but hearing only the hum and a little static, he hung up, automatically checked the coin return with one finger and without luck, then started down the tarmac road toward the theater, wondering what had got into him with his talk about a car.

Before the call to his parents, no thought of buying a car had entered his mind. Certainly the reasons he had given in support of buying a car were good reasons, but they did not account for the urgency with which he had delivered them. The urgency, he suddenly realized, had something to do with his promise at 1311 Elm. To get there on time tomorrow he would need to buy a car today. That was all there was to it. Though ten minutes earlier he had been ready to go to the laundromat and declare himself unfit for service, something in the phone call—he could not say what—had compelled him to change his mind.

In the theater Bennett found only Dicataldo and the thin attractive woman who was the stage manager. These two had already done half the job, but they cheered from the stage when Bennett arrived, coming through the doors from the lobby and down the aisle along the east wall.

As he joined them in the work—dismantling back-drops, sorting our props and costumes, carrying one thing and another to a van parked out back, sweeping, dusting, and so on—the conversation was spirited and various, but the main subject was Leskov and his sudden death. Apparently the news had spread rapidly, for it had already reached both Dicataldo and the stage manager before they set out for the theater this morning.

Merciless and irreverent on the subject, Dicataldo dominated the conversation and ended by declaring that, nevertheless, he intended definitely to go to the funeral this afternoon.

"The whole graduate school is going to be there," he said, "and I wouldn't miss it for the world. It's not every day you get a chance to see a son of a bitch like that to his grave and throw a little dirt on the box."

"I want you to know," said Bennett, after a pause, and taking Dicataldo by the arm, "that I have opinions and feelings about Leskov that are different from yours, and so in the future, specially in these days just after his death, if you value me as a friend, I ask you please to take my opinions and feelings about Leskov into account and try to keep from talking about him in this way in my presence."

The strange formality of this speech, and the fact that Bennett was trembling when he delivered it, took Dicataldo by surprise, and he searched Bennett's eyes for a moment, and then, apparently troubled, let the matter pass without further comment and walked off the stage through the wings and out the back door.

Bennett and the stage manager exchanged a glance. The stage manager said, "I think you hurt him."

"I know," said Bennett. "I just hope I haven't lost two friends today. I don't think I'm up to it."

But two minutes later Dicataldo returned in high spirits, waving a bottle of cheap red wine and three paper cups.

"Let's go down front and have a drink, folks!" he cried, limping exuberantly through the wings. "Uncle Anthony is here with the party!"

So the three students left their work, which was nearly done, and went down the short staircase at stage left into a dark house; then, illuminated only by the overflow of the light onstage, they proceeded up the center aisle, taking seats toward the rear, next to each other, with the stage manager in the middle, and began to drink the sharp cheap wine, wincing at its bite.

As Dicataldo was pouring a second round, Bennett began to tell about an idea that had come to him while he was helping to strike the set, an idea about a new play that he intended to begin writing during the winter recess.

"It's going to be a play about a guy who lives alone," he said, "an intellectual of some sort, about thirty years old, who wakes up one morning and can't remember most of what he did the night before. Since this is a new experience for him, he doesn't know what to make of it or what to expect, and at first he figures that if only he exerts himself a bit, his memory is bound to come back. But it doesn't. No matter what kind of mental tricks he plays on himself, the memory doesn't come back! And so, naturally, he starts to get worked up. Really worried. Starts to torture himself with all sorts of sinister fears about what he might have done the previous night. Crimes and perversions of every stamp, you see. Until, finally, he gets disgusted with all these filthy reveries, decides that he is not likely to get at the truth on his own, and goes out to visit some friends. Which at first seems like a good idea. Until he discovers that all of his friends have been plunged quite suddenly into private crises of their own . . . a regular frenzy of radical suffering in fact . . . and all apparently overnight! Understandably, in a situation like this, he is a little puzzled and doesn't feel too easy about introducing the subject of his memory problem. So he keeps it a secret. Goes among his friends like a spy, you see. Picks up a clue here, and a clue there, and, very circumspectly, bit by bit manages to put together a picture of the forgotten night and of what he did in it. This picture, though, gives him a bad turn. Because some of the things he did don't fit too well into the picture of the person he likes to believe himself to be."

"What kind of things are we talking about here?" said Dicataldo.

"Never mind about that."

"I want to know."

"Just leave it. I don't want to get into it right now. The main point about these things is that they are strange—strange to him, the hero . . . that they are things he ordinarily wouldn't think himself inclined to do."

"You mean things like the crimes and perversions that he'd been imagining in the morning."

250

"No, no. Nothing like that at all. That is just simple-minded knife-and-gun stuff. Family entertainment out of Euripides and the movies and the local emergency-room. The things that he actually did are much stranger. Subtler. They take him by surprise. You see? Bring him up short. Force him to consider the fact that he has certain impulses that he needs to get on more intimate terms with if he is going to keep his faculties intact. So he takes a look at these impulses and these peculiar things that he did and forgot . . . and after a bit he comes around to the view that the main danger to his life lies not in any of these impulses, or in any of these peculiar things he did and forgot, but rather in the forgetting, the forgetting itself. Because the forgetting, he suddenly realizes, disconnects. It disconnects bits and pieces of himself from each other. And disconnects all sorts of other things too. Even yesterday from today!"

"Wait," said Dicataldo. "Who does he say this to?"

"Nobody. Himself."

"It's a soliloquy."

"Right."

"Where is he when he delivers it."

"In his room. He's alone in his room. And it's night. Quite late. He's just got home after a hard day with his friends. And he's standing by his bed. Dead tired. And at the same time he is afraid to lie down."

"Why?"

"Because . . ."

"Wait. Because he's afraid that if he goes to sleep, he'll forget again, right?"

"Right. Exactly."

251

"This is good. Then what?"

"Then he has a visitor."

"Somebody knocks on the door."

"No, no, this is not the sort of character who knocks on doors."

"He just barges in, then. Because he's rude."

"No, he's not rude. He is supernatural. And he just quite simply *appears*."

"Christ."

"Give me a minute on this, Dicataldo."

"What the hell do you need a supernatural character for? You had one in the Greenfield play, and it was ridiculous!"

"Which character are you talking about?"

"Time. The Time character."

"Oh, right. Time. I forgot about him. Well . . . this one is different."

"What's he like, then."

"I don't know exactly . . . I don't have an image worked out yet . . . I guess he might have, like, say, enormous wings . . . and these, like, very cunning expressive hands . . . and maybe he should have claws on his feet . . . and he should have this very rich snaky voice, full of echoes . . . I don't know . . . the details aren't all that important . . . the main thing about this character is that there should be some very disturbing ambiguity about him, about whether he comes from Heaven or from Hell, and that he should convey a sense of really terrific power, so that the moment he appears on the stage, everybody gets a chill at the back of the neck."

"All right. I get the picture. But, look . . . what do you need him for? You were doing just fine up to this point."

"I need him to show the way out."

"The way out of what?"

"The disconnection problem."

"And how is he going to do that?"

"He is going to present the hero with a task."

"A task."

"Yes. Exactly what task I don't know yet. I know only that it will be something in the line of benevolence, but dreary and difficult, something to do with disease and excrement and death, and that the hero will have to do it every day over a period of many days, maybe a year or so, and that he will commit himself to it as if his life depended on it."

"Does it?"

"I don't know yet. Probably."

"Why can't you have an ordinary person turn up and present the hero with this task?"

"Because I want the hero to be knocked out . . . fascinated . . . trembling . . . really *struck*."

"Why?"

"I just do! And if the character who presents the task is just an ordinary person, some guy who just 'turns up,' as you say, and 'knocks on the door,' our trembling hero is going to look like a clown."

"So what?"

"So I don't want him to look like a clown! Can't you understand that?"

"Not entirely. But it's your play."

"That's right. It is."

"So then what? I mean, after the guy with the wings shows the way out, what happens next? I suppose he vanishes, right?"

"Right. He vanishes."

"Then what?"

"I can't say yet. My idea is that hopefully this new task will make the hero a better man—that it will keep his faculties intact and his feet on the ground and help him get to sleep without fear. But who knows? It could just as likely turn out that the subversive forces creating all the inner disturbances, the fits of amnesia and so on, will prove to be irresistible . . . or, worse, that the task itself will be too much for him and, in the long run, will sink him like a stone. I don't know! Maybe I'll know later. I need some time. I need to make some notes . . . to get something down on the page . . . some of the particulars . . . the characters and the landscape . . . and also maybe a few generalities . . . like the forgetting . . . and the remembering . . . mainly the forgetting and the remembering. Is any of this making sense? What do you think?"

At this point the stage manager took Bennett's hand and held it and smiled at him, and her smile and her hand surprised him and stirred him, and suddenly he felt very good, very good, and he looked into the paper cup, which contained about a half-pint of wine, and he drank it in one long draft; after which Dicataldo promptly filled the cup again; and again Bennett drank the wine, but this time he managed only half the cup before a numbness began to come over his whole body, and he lost the thread of what he had been thinking about, and he felt himself drifting away, away from everything, everything, even the warm pressure of the stage manager's hand, until at last he fell into a deep sleep, a deep dreamless sleep, like a dark empty theater, with all the props, the set, the cast, the crew, and the audience itself, posted outside the doors, ready to come in.

John Slidell